THE FIRST TIME DAD'S GUIDE TO RAISING A TODDLER

A FATHER'S HANDBOOK ON CONQUERING TANTRUMS, SLEEP WOES, POTTY TRAINING, AND BOUNDARY BATTLES WHILE AVOIDING PARENTAL BURNOUT

REMINGTON JAMES

CONTENTS

INTRODUCTION

It was like watching images of an exoplanet sent to Earth by the James Webb Space Telescope. Or seeing a gymnast pull off a front handspring followed by two front somersaults with a half-twist, the most difficult move in the sport. Or watching David Copperfield do a magic trick that made thousands of people gasp in astonishment.

My daughter, Ashley, was taking her first steps at just eleven months old!

Let me tell you, it was the proudest moment of my life, including that time I ate ten hotdogs in under six minutes and didn't throw up. The baby books said that most children walk between nine and 15 months. So surely that put my child in one of the upper percentiles, right?

Best of all, I was there to see it. Most dads miss these first moments because we're out at work when it happens. A lot of moms miss them, too, but after they have a child, many professional women cut down their hours or even quit their jobs entirely to be full-time mothers. (Yes, this is one of the best-kept secrets in the modern world). But dads? We just work harder to provide for our family.

I had always intended to be a hands-on father from the moment Jenny told me she was pregnant. I spent those nine months not only learning everything I could about pregnancy and baby care (see my last book, *7 Chapters Every First Time Dad Needs to Read*) but also arranging my businesses so I could work more from home. I still didn't get everything right, but I did the baby care (and pregnant wife care) thing better than I would have otherwise.

But then I watched Ashley take those first few steps and plop down on her butt with a surprised look on her face. As Jenny and I applauded, I realized in that moment that while I knew how to take care of a baby, I didn't know how to care for a toddler. Yes, *obviously*, I should have read up about toddlers just as I had about babies. Yes, a toddler poses fresh challenges. And a father will face unique challenges from a mother, and I should have read up on that.So, why wasn't I ready for toddlerhood? Well, I had just been too busy and tired for the past ten months!

Taking care of baby Ashley was a lot of work. I changed diapers, bathed her, fed her, and put her to sleep. But suddenly, I realized that had been the easy part. After all, babies only sleep, eat, and poop. They don't walk, talk, and try to get their own way like a toddler. How on earth was I going to handle that? I knew how to take care of a baby. Taking care of a little person was a different ball game altogether.

So, that evening, as soon as Ashley was tired of showing off her newfound ability, I did what I usually do: I started looking for information.

One of the first sources I found stated that "changes in the first three years of life are rapid and immense with infant-toddler development categorized by dramatic brain and physical growth, an accelerated acquisition of language skills, intense responses to stimuli, and an extreme reliance on adult relationships."[1] I didn't comprehend most of that sentence, but what I understood didn't exactly reassure me. What was I supposed to *do*? That's what I wanted to know.

Another source stated that "as children grow from infants to toddlers, they undergo several major rapid developmental changes that support their increasing independence. First, during this period, a child moves from crawling to walking and running."[2] Running? What the hell did they mean, *running*?

Clearly unconcerned about panicked parents, the authors went on: "This newfound mobility allows children to explore with increasing curiosity. Some parents may find their child now 'gets into everything' and child-proofing the environment becomes a must."[3]

At least I had already baby-proofed all the electrical sockets and cupboard door handles. I turned back to Google and searched how to stop toddlers from turning on the stove, opening fridge doors, and climbing up wardrobes.

So now, you new dads are going to benefit from all my hours of research and years of being a father to a toddler. I'm going to help save you time, money, and, most of all, energy. I suspect that's why you're reading this book in the first place. What prompted you to seek guidance on parenting a toddler? Was it that sleepless night when you realized that soothing a crying toddler isn't quite the same as soothing a newborn because, you know, monsters? Maybe it was when you started trying to potty train, and you realized that a. this stage requires unlimited patience; b. you must not only cajole but persuade; and c. toddler poop, unlike baby poop, stinks.

In this book, you'll find many tips and tricks, from feeding your toddler (it's no longer as easy as putting a bottle in their mouth), putting them to sleep (rocking and lullabies won't do it anymore), getting them to do what you want (no, giving orders doesn't work) and, most of all, building a relationship with this new little person.

Parenthood presents a unique set of challenges, especially for a new dad. The sleepless nights, the endless crying, the unpredictability of tantrums—these are experiences that can make even the most confident of fathers feel uncertain. But you can stop worrying—I'm here to help (and I'm not from the government). Many new dads have walked this path before you and come out on the other side with a deep sense of accomplishment and a wealth of wonderful memories.

You might wonder, "can I really handle all this?" The answer is a resounding "Yes!" You have within you the capacity to cope, to learn, and to adapt. Your role as a father is vital, and the challenges you face are opportunities for growth, learning, and an even deeper love for your child than you thought possible. Just as your toddler is learning and developing, so are you. Every sleepless night, every bit of food flung on the floor, every tear wiped away —they're all part of the journey that will shape you into the amazing dad you're destined to become.

I am telling you this from experience and many, many hours of research. From the moment she was born, I loved my daughter more than anything else in the world. But I realized that the love was one-way. She depended totally on me and her mother, which made her instinctive responses to us even more powerful than love.

But, once she was a toddler learning to walk and who would soon talk, I realized that her responses to me would change into true interaction. What would she think of her daddy? Would she find I was the most handsome man in the world, as daughters tend to until they get sensible (unless, of course, they're George Clooney's daughter)? Or would she fear my nose? Was it better to speak to her in my normal voice, or was there some sort of *father speak* I had to learn?

I'm going to answer all these questions and more. I'm also going to tell you what questions (or, rather, what answers) *aren't* important. What I quickly discovered when I read books and articles and watched videos about baby care was that a lot of the advice seemed aimed at stressing out parents. This was even truer for toddler care. I guess the idea is to scare parents and then offer them solutions to take away that fear. But the stress remains since parents worry that they might not use the solutions effectively. I think this is even truer for dads than for moms because we live in a society that tells moms they're wonderful and, all too often, sends the opposite message about dads. (Just think of all those sitcoms where the father's failures are a running joke.)

The fact is, fatherhood is a unique journey filled with its own set of triumphs and trials. While parenting advice is abundant, much of it doesn't speak directly to fathers. That is the main reason I wrote this book. I wanted to recognize the distinctive role fathers play and offer solutions tailored to our perspective. Whether it's conquering the stormy seas of tantrums or emerging victorious in the potty-training battlefield, this book will be your trusted ally. I want to empower you to be the confident, caring dad your little one looks up to—a dad who can weather any storm and find joy in the journey.

This book will equip you with the tools and knowledge to be the loving, supportive dad your daughter or son needs. Embrace this journey with courage, wisdom, and an unwavering sense of joy because every step you take will shape memories you will cherish for a lifetime.

PART I

BUILDING A STRONG FOUNDATION

1

THE ADVENTURE OF RAISING A GROWING TODDLER

You know how sometimes you're sleeping, and you dream that something's weighing down your chest? It's an unnerving feeling. I remember that happened to me when Ashley was two years, three months, and four days old. I know how old she was because, as I struggled awake, I found her sitting on my chest, looking down at me.

"Morning, Punchabear," I said.

"Morning, Daddy," she answered. She paused. "Sleep good?"

"I was until a strange creature came and sat on me like I was a chair."

She watched me for a few more seconds, then smiled, slid off me and down the bed, and ran to the corner to play with her dolls. She didn't get my joke, but she knew I had made one. After I got up and had my coffee, I wrote about what had happened in my *Daughter Journal* on my computer. (I had also started a separate journal for my son, who at the time was two months and two days old.) My college acquaintance Roger, who was the only one in my class who was already married with a child, had advised me to keep a journal about my children. In my first book, I described how I turned to him for guidance about being a new dad after Ashley was born. We've been good friends since.

"You'll take a million photos, but you won't remember what you thought about what they were doing when you took them," Roger explained. "Also, when they're older, they'll want to know what their first word was, when they started teething, and why you ruined their life. Your journal will have the answers."

"I'll ruin their lives?" I asked, immediately worried because that's how I am.

Roger laughed. "Not likely. But you'll find a lot of articles and books that will tell you, if you don't do everything the authors say, it will scar your children for life."

This turned out to be true, and I'll deal with that later in this chapter. I was glad I took Roger's advice, though, because the journal not only let me go back to what would become precious memories (like Ashley sitting on my chest to contemplate her Daddy) but also tracked her and her brother's development from babyhood to toddlerhood.

MILESTONES ARE NOT SET IN STONE

Once they're one to three years old, we consider babies toddlers. They move around a lot more (and really fast!); they become self-aware (which you know by them putting their toes in their mouth when you tell them not to); and they also become more curious about their surroundings (especially breakable things). According to the Centers for Disease Control and Prevention, toddlers "imitate the behavior of others, especially adults and older children."[1] As soon as Ashley and Tyler turned two, I started washing the dishes, vacuuming, and doing the taxes in front of them. Because everybody said that it's never too early to teach your children about life, right?

Here's what distinguishes a toddler from an infant.[2] Foremost, a toddler is more active; they do more than just feeding, crying, and pooping. (Whoever guessed you would look back wistfully at those simpler times?) They use words, and you may regret ever encouraging them to talk. And, of course, they stand up and take steps, which is when you really start to worry. They play games and want to do things by themselves. They get interested in objects and start demanding you give things to them, no doubt practicing for getting the keys to the car. And they get angry, often at being unable to communicate with you—a state that will only get worse when they're teenagers. (Let me tell you now, I'm *not* looking forward to writing *that* book.)

Anyway, here's a list of what your toddler should do when they're about **one year** to **18 months** old.[3] As I go through this list, I want you to keep the sub-heading above in mind. The timeline for when a child should talk, walk, and give you heart attacks is quite variable. Ashley hit some right on time, was ahead of others, and didn't do other things until after she was supposed to (according to the experts).

- Using words
- Pointing to objects
- Pushing, pulling, and dumping objects
- Stacking two blocks
- Handing objects to others
- Playing peek-a-boo
- Crawling strongly
- Standing without support, sitting upright
- Taking steps
- Hiding and finding objects
- Noticing other children
- Playing with blocks and puzzles
- Climbing into chairs

Again, I want to emphasize that there's a lot of variability with these indicators. Ashley said her first word when she was 13 months old, but my son Tyler didn't do anything but babble till he was 18 months old (although his mother insists she could understand what he was saying as early as 11 months old).

At 18 months to two years, your toddler may:

- Use eight or more words
- Point to pictures in books
- Scribble
- Use a spoon and a cup
- Walk quickly
- Show interest in using the toilet
- Walk forward and backward
- Roll a large ball back-and-forth
- Stoop and squat
- Turn pages of books
- Use two- to three-word sentences
- Point to body parts
- Sing and dance
- Imitate parent activities
- Have tantrums

And, no, I don't know what "show an interest in using the toilet" means. I'll just say that potty training is probably the most challenging part of toddler parenting—though it's possible that's just me. Don't worry; I have an entire chapter to help you get through this easier than I did— skip ahead to chapter five. As for tantrums, Ashley had some, and Tyler had none.

ON YOUR CHILD'S MIND

In handling my daughter and son in their toddler stage, I found it useful to learn some child psychology—i.e., try to understand how their minds work. There are several useful nuggets of information about child psychology that are based on the theories of Swiss Psychologist Jean Piaget.

Through observation of children, Piaget proposed they move through four different stages of learning.[4] These are:

1. **Sensorimotor stage** (birth to two years): In this stage, babies build an understanding of the world by touching, grasping, watching, and listening.
2. **Preoperational stage** (two to seven years old): At this stage, children use language and develop their capacity for abstract thinking. They also begin symbolic play (playing pretend) by talking about imaginary acts or things and drawing pictures.
3. **Concrete operational stage** (seven to eleven years old): Children learn logical, concrete rules about objects, such as height, weight, and volume.
4. **Formal operational stage** (twelve years old and up): Adolescents learn logical rules to understand abstract concepts and solve problems.

In this book, we're only concerned with toddlers, so I will mainly focus on stages one and two. In Piaget's first stage, your toddler is:

1. Learning about the world through basic actions such as sucking, grasping, looking, and listening
2. Learning that things continue to exist even when they cannot be seen (object permanence)
3. Realizing that they are separate beings from the people and objects around them
4. Realizing that their actions can cause things to happen in the world around them

The cognitive development during this stage happens pretty quickly. The leaps your child makes will amaze you. In fact, Piaget may have underestimated how fast children develop. Psychologist Robin Dawes notes that "Subsequent research has demonstrated that this progression is far from orderly and that Piaget may have confused an appreciation of the world as it is with an ability of verbalize that appreciation."[5] So, even infants appear to understand object permanence and even numbers (albeit only at the level of one, two, and three, which I find is still pretty impressive).

One interesting reason it seems to us parents that our children are just leaping from one stage to another is that children actually conceal their growing abilities until they decide to express them. A father-mother duo of psychologists discovered this by hanging a recording device on their child's crib and hearing her saying words she never used around them.here's what you can expect in the preoperational stage from your toddler:

- Their vocabulary grows rapidly, and they begin to use words to express their thoughts and feelings.
- They engage in pretend play, using objects to represent other things, such as a banana for a telephone.
- They become egomaniacs—i.e., they can't see things from other people's perspective.

I cannot overemphasize this last point enough. Understanding that our toddlers are egomaniacs is key to effectively handling their otherwise inexplicable behavior. This is why Piaget was so important because, until him, everyone assumed children were just small adults. Unfortunately, a lot of parents still treat their children like this, which can actually result in harm to children. Children not only need their parents' love but also their guidance.

We need to understand that two-year-olds are not egomaniacs because they're self-centered but simply because their brains haven't developed enough to understand what's called the "theory of mind." This is the understanding that other people think differently from them. (And, yes, a lot of politicians and intellectuals appear to have never developed past the two-year-old stage.) It's also useful for parents to expect their toddlers to be disagreeable and even aggressive. "The most violent age is not adolescence but toddlerhood," writes the scholar Steven Pinker. "In a recent large study, almost half the boys just past the age of two, and a smaller percentage of girls, engaged in hitting, biting, and kicking."[6]

People have dubbed this stage the *Terrible Twos* for a few reasons, and as parents, we have a duty to guide our toddlers through it until they understand they are not the only beings in the world.

Here are some tips on how you, as a dad, can make this phase easier.

Daddy's Home

Play is how toddlers learn, and, generally speaking, fathers like playing with their children more than moms.[7] (Why not? We're big kids ourselves, as our wives frequently tell us.)

When we play with our kids, we help them explore and express their emotions and, with fathers especially, help them learn how to *manage* their feelings. This sets the foundation for self-control and getting along with other people—essential skills for success in later life. You can even use play to get them to eat healthily. We had Tyler's "Great Vegetable Expedition" when, faced with a plate of vegetables, he shook his head with a firm "No!" So, I told him the broccoli were tiny trees and carrots were orange rockets. He had lots of fun crashing the rockets into the trees and then eating both.

As Dad, your role is to help fix things, whether it's a broken toy or a skinned knee. (And, yes, you must kiss both.) Your toddler will observe how you express your own feelings, so you should be a good role model. If they're angry or frustrated, it's even more important that you display calm and understanding.

Remember that your toddler, because they're becoming self-aware, will experience new feelings, such as fear, embarrassment, and envy. This makes them more likely to cry, yell, or even hit when they don't get their way. Being little dictators, they won't understand why they can't get whatever, whether it's a piece of chocolate or Poland. It's up to you to explain why and calm them down even when they don't understand your explanation. (Explain, anyway.)

By the time children turn three or thereabout, most toddlers start to feel emotions like guilt and shame. Listening to them, giving them reassurance, and telling them when they do something wrong can help them understand these new feelings.

Playing with your child enables you, as a dad, to nurture learning and foster connections.[8] Offering gentle guidance during play, without assuming complete control or being overly restrictive, can help a child master various skills faster, as compared to solitary play (though it's also important to let them play by themselves). Games, almost by definition, teach children about leadership, decision-making, resilience, communication, creativity, and focus.

Fathers can further enhance playtime through a teaching approach known as scaffolding—i.e., allowing children to build upon their existing knowledge. For example, if a child has learned to stack blocks, a father can encourage them to experiment with different and imaginative stacking methods, build taller structures, or, best of all, destroy stacks.

Here are five strategies you can use to help your child's development through play:

1. *Pay attention.* Observe and listen closely to your child's interests and enthusiasm during playtime, responding with encouragement and even criticism.
2. *Engage in child-led play.* Embrace the child's leadership within the game, allowing them to take initiative.
3. *Foster curiosity.* Avoid imposing strict rules or guidelines. Go with the flow; be a jazz playmate.
4. *Enhance skills.* Encourage activities that refine motor skills (e.g., crawling), mental skills (e.g., counting), or emotional control. (e.g., "Why do you like that? I think it's silly.")

5. *Ask open-ended questions.* Use open-ended questions to stimulate critical thinking. Examples include "what happens when we try this?" or "what does this remind you of?"

All this sets the foundation for your future relationship with your child. But I don't want you to think that if you cannot do these things, you will have a poor relationship with them or traumatize them for life. The following section is a warning against parenting "experts" who continually warn you about bad parenting.

DON'T WORRY, BE HAPPY PARENTING

In doing research for this book, I found that most parenting articles and books took a dire tone about what would happen to your child if you didn't DO THE RIGHT THING. Without quite saying so, the implication was always that if you didn't follow this expert advice, your child would have depression, never go to college, and vote for a party that the expert didn't support. One source stated that "early nurturing care reduces the likelihood of risky and antisocial behavior later on, and the costs they bring to individuals and society. Early relationships have long-lasting impacts, not only through the lifetime of a child but onto subsequent generations."[9]

Entire generations, no less. It's like a Biblical curse.

So, let me make it clear: some children who have experienced extreme child abuse are affected in their adult lives by this early childhood experience. And, since you are reading this book, it's safe to assume that you are not a parent who would either commit such abuse or put their child in a situation where such abuse could occur for any length of time.

The premise of the quoted passage is that our experiences in life can affect our children's children. But this is contradictory since the passage also asserts that relationships (i.e., environment) can overcome generational influences. The fact is, the burgeoning field of epigenetics shows that only extreme conditions alter an individual's genes in ways that can be passed on through the sex chromosomes, and even then, those effects vanish by the second generation.[10]

Here's another passage from the same website: "Science tells us that a child's experiences from conception through their first five years will go on to shape their next 50. It tells us that the kind of children we raise today will reflect the kind of world we will live in tomorrow. It tells us that investing in the start of life is not an indulgence, but economically, socially and psychologically vital to a prosperous society."

This implies that our destiny, for good or ill, is set from the time we are five years old. There is no possibility for us to take action to change ourselves. Not only is this pessimistic, but it is also wrong: science says no such thing.[11]

Being a parent is supposed to be your greatest source of purpose, meaning, and fun. If it becomes a chore, then you're doing it wrong. Will you make mistakes? For sure. Will this make your child a failure in life? Certainly not. If they fail, it will be for other reasons. This is also true if they succeed.

You focus on having a good relationship with them and keeping them safe. That's what parenting is all about.

KEY TAKEAWAYS

- Toddlers have increased mobility, self-awareness, and curiosity.
- Piaget's cognitive development stages help you understand why your toddler is not a little angel.
- Fathers contribute to their child's development by engaging in play and helping toddlers manage their emotions.
- Making mistakes won't scar your child for life.

In the next chapter, I look at ways to communicate effectively with your toddler and how to understand what they're trying to tell you.

2

THE LANGUAGE OF LOVE

B ack in the 1950s, most American first-graders learned to read from a book series called—I kid you not—*Dick and Jane*.[1] And, no, I don't think the boy's name was accidental—an equivalent British series first published by Ladybird books in 1964 named the boy character "Peter."

Both series were boring and bad but sold millions of copies. I guess the parents were buying them, and children didn't backtalk in those days. How times have changed! The reason the original books were bad is that they drastically underestimated how many words children knew.

The *Dick and Jane* readers for six-year-olds had about three hundred words, eight- to nine-year-olds had one thousand words, while the 11- to -12-year-olds got a book with a whopping 4000 words.[2] Similarly, the Ladybird books for "a budding reader of primary school age, from 3 to 5 years old...uses the 12 keywords which are used repeatedly: "Here is Peter," "Peter is here," "Here is Jane," "Jane is here," "I like Peter," "I like Jane."[3]However, as psycholinguist Steven Pinker points out, "an average six-year-old commands about 13,000 words (notwithstanding those dull, dull *Dick and Jane* reading primers, which were based on ridiculously lowball estimates)." Children learn words at twelve months. That means they learn about ten new words every ninety waking minutes.[4] Imagine if you had to learn 40 words in a foreign language every day. Even if you could do it, you'd have little time for any other activity. So, at the very least, you've got to keep up with your toddler's growing language skills.

TODDLER TALK

By the time your toddler is two years old, they'll be using words more often than gestures (or tears) when they want to tell you something.[5] This is because their vocabulary (and brains) are now developed enough to communicate what they want.They graduate from single words to two- and three-word phrases. Even as a baby, Tyler was always determined to communicate exactly what he wanted. One time, when he was about two years old, he kept pointing at the fridge and saying, "juice." I kept giving him different juice choices, but he kept shaking his head and saying "no." Finally, I realized he wanted apple juice specifically.

From then on, I made sure to always have apple juice in the fridge for him.

He would also always say, "Me do it," whenever he wanted to do something by himself. It was his way of asserting his independence and showing us he could do things on his own.

So, expect to hear things like, "More milk," "Want juice," "Go bye-bye," "Give me ball," and even "Daddy, get in car." As I'm going to do throughout this book, remember toddlers have a pretty wide range of normal development, so you shouldn't worry if they aren't at this level at two years of age. That said, if your toddler speaks but then stops, consult your pediatrician or a speech therapist.

Even though your toddler will use words to ask for things most of the time, they'll use all possible means to communicate, including flinging stuff. Once they're using a combination of communication strategies (gestures, sounds, and words) and using words and phrases more often, they're right on track. Often, they'll learn the words for their favorite things first. You should also remember your toddler knows a lot more words than they can say. As with the Dick and Jane publishers, most baby sites still underestimate this number. "It will be hard to actually calculate the number of words they know or understand because the number is so large. If you were to calculate the number of words two-year-olds know, you would count well over 1,000 words."[6]

Toddlers should also be able to follow instructions requiring more than one action. For example, if you tell them, "Put the toy down and close the door," or "Find the red crayon and give it to me," or "Pick up the toys and put them in the box," they will understand you perfectly well. This doesn't mean they'll actually obey you, but it's good practice for when they become teenagers.

You can also expect them to become little journalists, asking questions like who, what, when, where, why, and how. "What's that, Daddy?" "Who is that, Daddy?"Just because your toddler is saying words doesn't mean that you will understand what they're saying, though. Knowing a word is one thing; saying it clearly is another. When my daughter Ashley was learning to talk, she had a hard time pronouncing certain sounds. Instead of getting frustrated, she would come up with her own words for things. For example, she couldn't say "spaghetti," so she called it "pisghetti" instead.

The rule of thumb is once you can understand about half of what your toddler says, they're on track. I've put together a list of things you should look out for:

Which sounds should you be listening for?

☐ Pronounces most Consonant Sounds: P, B, T, D, K, G, M, N, H, W, F
☐ Vowel Sounds: can pronounce all the vowel sounds

☐ You can understand 50-75% of what your child says
☐ May leave consonant sounds off the ends of words

Expression Skills (Expressive Language)

☐ Seems to have a word for just about everything
☐ Uses words from all the basic grammar categories: nouns, verbs, adjectives, and adverbs.
☐ Says two- and three-word phrases.
☐ Uses words to express their wants, needs, ideas, and feelings.

Understanding Skills (Receptive Language)

☐ Answers some "wh" questions, especially what, who, and why. (Be warned: this last one is going to become their favorite word from ages three to 12.)
☐ Follows directions that have one or two actions.
☐ Listens to your commands in safety situations: *No! Stop!*
☐ Has back-and-forth "conversations," even if you don't understand what they're saying. Just smile and say, "Okay," like you do with your wife when she's talking about curtains.
☐ Learns new words when introduced to new things.

Social Communication Skills

☐ Chats with familiar children and adults.

☐ Can do the same activity for at least several minutes.

☐ Can talk about what's going to happen.

☐ Understands other people's tone of voice.

☐ Knows how to get your attention or ask for help when needed.

DADDY TALKS FUNNY

As a parent, you've probably already started using the speech pattern called *parentese*. (It used to be called "motherese" until linguists finally figured out that Dads used it, too.) Pinker describes *parentese* as "slower, more exaggerated in pitch, more directed to the here and now, and more grammatical [with] a rise and fall contour for approving, a set of sharp, staccato bursts for prohibiting, a rising pattern for directing attention, and smooth, low legato murmurs for comforting."[7] When your child was still an infant, you may have used a higher-pitched tone of voice, simple sentences, and stretched out your vowels. ("Hehhh-looo Tyyleeer")

It turns out that babies prefer this type of speech over typical adult speech, perhaps because the exaggerated sounds help them learn the sounds of their native language. *Parentese* isn't the same as "baby talk," though— in fact, they are completely different. While baby talk is a nonsense language (the classic "goo-goo-gaga"), *parentese* uses actual words and follows grammatical rules.

By the time your child becomes a toddler, you won't be using *parentese* so much, but you will still speak differently to her or him than you would an adult or even a teenager. Some useful principles when conversing with your toddler are:Pause to let them respond when you tell them something.

- Listen to what they're saying and ask them to explain some part of it (e.g., "My dolly doesn't like potato, and she says it's icky." "What do you mean, icky?")
- Explain what you're doing. For instance, if you're making fried eggs, describe the steps and why you're doing them.

The quantity and quality of language exposure in the first three years of a child's life can greatly vary. Quantity simply refers to the number of words they hear every day, while quality refers to the variety of words. So, one way to help your child master a language is by talking about your daily activities. This helps children associate words with objects and actions. For example, while preparing a meal, you could say, "I'm cutting up the carrots for our soup. They're bright orange and crunchy!" Or, while going for a walk, you could say, "We're walking to the park now. Can you hear the birds singing? Look at the big, green trees!"

Reading with your child also has long-term benefits for their language development. Take advantage of quiet moments to read together, whether it's before bed or while waiting for the bus. Have your toddler turn the pages and describe what they see. Ask them questions about the pictures or see if they want to tell you the story themselves.

Here are some other ways to help your child gain high-level language abilities:

- *Sing and play music.* Research has shown that an enriched musical environment in infancy can promote the development of communication skills.
- *Encourage language development through play.* Engage in dramatic play with your child to help them develop their language skills.
- *Use language learning apps.* There are many apps available that can help children learn language, such as Duolingo, Memrise, Busuu, and Drops.
- *Play language-based games.* Games like Scrabble, Pictionary, or Charades can help children develop their vocabulary and communication skills.
- *Tell jokes.* Telling age-appropriate jokes can help foster good humor and creativity in children and encourages wordplay and imagination.

Whatever approach you choose (and that your child finds interesting), the most important thing is to provide a rich language environment and to engage with them in a variety of activities that promote language development.

TEN TODDLER TALK STRATEGIES

Effective communication from you helps lay the foundation for a child's language development, cognitive growth, and social interaction skills. As parents and caregivers, our role in fostering language proficiency is pivotal. Here are 10 strategies you can use to facilitate language acquisition and linguistic enrichment in children.

1. *Model clear speech.* Speaking clearly and enunciating words helps children learn the correct pronunciation and articulation of sounds. By modeling good speech, you provide a template for effective communication that your child can mimic. This helps expand their vocabulary but also encourages them to express themselves clearly.
2. *Offer repetition and expansion.* Repeating what your child says not only shows active listening but also builds their confidence in expressing themselves. In my personal experience, dads are more likely than moms to use more complex words (partly because we're not as familiar with our children's vocabulary, partly because we don't care), which helps broaden their understanding and language repertoire. For example, responding to "Want

juice?" with "I have apple juice. Do you want apple juice?" creates dialogue and fosters language development.

3. *Embrace both baby talk and adult words.* A balanced approach to language use involves incorporating both baby talk and adult words. While using simplified language aids in comprehension, introducing advanced terms encourages vocabulary growth. Balancing phrases like "It's time for din-din. We'll have dinner now" helps children recognize and associate the adult term with the simplified version, which enhances their linguistic competency.

4. *Provide picture categorization and creativity.* Visual aids are powerful tools for language learning. Creating categories such as "things to ride on," "things to eat," and "things to play with" using cut-out pictures stimulates cognitive organization. Crafting whimsical combinations of pictures, such as a dog behind the wheel of a car, fosters imagination and prompts discussions about incongruities, further enhancing language exploration.

5. *Question and play the Yes-No game.* Asking questions is an interactive method to boost language development. Engaging in the Yes-No game—posing questions like "Are you Marty?" or "Can pigs fly?"—not only encourages critical thinking but also hones listening skills.

Encouraging children to plan their questions fosters creativity and promotes a deeper understanding of conversational dynamics.

6. *Offer choices.* Giving your child choices fosters a sense of independence, bolsters confidence, and encourages them to make decisions. Questions like "Do you want an apple or an orange?" or "Do you want to wear your red shirt or your blue shirt?" or "Do you want to play for the Dodgers or Rangers?" encourage the expression of preferences and teach the concept of decision-making, all while enhancing their language skills. Unless, that is, they choose the Rangers.

7. *Expand vocabulary through body parts.* Engaging children in discussions about body parts is an engaging way to expand vocabulary. Naming body parts and explaining their functions—such as "This is my nose. I can smell flowers, brownies, and soap"—adds a sensory dimension to language learning. Associating words with sensory experiences deepens comprehension and memory retention.

8. *Honor the rhythmic power of songs and nursery rhymes.* Singing simple songs and reciting nursery rhymes not only introduces children to the musicality of language but also reinforces the rhythmic patterns of speech. The repetition and rhyme schemes in these verses aid in memorization and enhance phonological

awareness, laying the groundwork for reading and language skills. Ashey is pretty good at making up rap songs, and I credit this to the many hours she spent as a one-year-old listening to The Wheels on the Bus Go Round and Round.

9. *Explore through familiar objects.* Encouraging children to explore and describe familiar objects fosters creativity and linguistic development. Placing objects in a box and having the child identify and describe them—such as "This is my ball. I bounce it. I play with it"—helps expand their vocabulary and sentence complexity, which enhances their ability to communicate their experiences.

10. *Engage in storytelling through pictures.* Here's where your smartphone comes in truly useful. Show your child photos of people and places your child is familiar with and guide him or her to make up a story. This activity not only enhances language skills but also strengthens cognitive abilities and a love for storytelling. And a child who becomes an adult who can tell stories will always have an advantage in life because we all love stories.

FEEL ME?

In teaching toddlers to communicate effectively, empathy is a key trait that you must nurture. Empathy, the ability to understand and share the feelings of others, is a skill that shapes not only effective communication but also lays the foundation for valuable life skills.[8]

Empathy equips children with the capacity to comprehend the emotions and experiences of those around them. By recognizing how their actions can impact others and appreciating the reasons behind various emotions, children navigate the intricacies of human interaction. This skill is invaluable in their developmental years and well into adulthood. Empathy is necessary for:

- *Building Strong Relationships and Security*: As children learn to acknowledge and understand the feelings of others, they create a foundation of trust and security within their relationships. This emotional security, in turn, enhances their receptiveness to learning and their overall social integration.
- *Encouraging Tolerance and Acceptance:* Empathy encourages children to recognize the diversity of emotions and experiences that individuals may have. This recognition fosters tolerance and acceptance, teaching children to embrace varying perspectives.
- *Promoting Mental Health*: Empathy is closely linked to emotional intelligence, which is a crucial aspect of good mental health. Children who can understand their emotions and empathize with others are better equipped to manage their own

feelings, navigate challenges, and seek support when needed.

- *Creating Social Harmony and Reducing Bullying*: An empathetic child is more likely to respect the emotions and boundaries of their peers. This can lead to healthier social dynamics and a decreased likelihood of engaging in or tolerating bullying behavior.

The benefits of nurturing empathy during childhood extend well beyond the formative years. As these empathetic children grow into adults, they carry with them a set of skills that can contribute to personal and professional success. Empathetic adults tend to have better interpersonal skills, making it easier to build rapport with colleagues, clients, and customers.[9]

Fostering empathy in your toddler is a foundational step toward effective communication and personal growth. By understanding the importance of empathy and its long-lasting effects, fathers can help the emotional intelligence and overall well-being of the next generation.

KEY TAKEAWAYS

- Your toddler typically develops language skills quickly.
- Foster this ability by talking to them continually.

- Language is the foundation of empathy, which helps them to become successful adults.

Communicating well with your toddler at this stage has one tremendous advantage: it will help you deal with those dreaded temper tantrums. Turn the page to the next chapter—if you dare.

PART II

TACKLING COMMON CHALLENGES

3

MELTDOWNS MADE
MANAGEABLE

B efore your child transitions from infant to toddler, both you and your partner should undergo surgery to eliminate your sense of embarrassment. I promise you, your child *will* embarrass you: with your family, with your friends, and especially in public.

Most strangers find babies cute and will tolerate their crying, messy eating, and even pooping (once it's in a diaper). But badly behaved toddlers get far less leeway. From commenting on Aunt Judy's chin wart, taking off all their clothes when you have friends over for dinner, or banging their heads on the supermarket floor because, *"I want the curvy pasta, not the straight one!"* You're going to have to train them how to behave (and, yes, I mean "train," just like a puppy).

Here's why you need to not feel embarrassed by anything your child does: because when we feel embarrassed, we get angry. The first and most important rule of controlling your toddler's tantrums is: *Do not get angry.*

"A common mistake that parents make when disciplining is that they don't control their own emotions," writes Britney Watkins in her modestly titled book *The Ultimate Guide to Parenting.* "When you lose your temper at your child, you, in essence, abdicate your emotional responsibility and give it to the youngest and least mature person in your household.[1]

Clinical psychologist Jordan Peterson, in his bestselling book *12 Rules for Life*, has a chapter titled "Do Not Let Your Children Do Anything That Makes You Dislike Them." Peterson's argument is straightforward: "It is the primary duty of parents to make their children socially desirable. That will provide the child with opportunity, self-regard, and security...You love your kids, after all. If their actions make you dislike them, think what an effect they have on other people, who care much less about them than you..."[2]

So, helping your child to stop throwing tantrums is good for them and even better for you. The first step is understanding what causes them to have a meltdown.

OURS IS NOT TO REASON WHY KIDS THROW TANTRUMS

If you have a toddler, you most likely have a tantrum story. Here's one of mine.*When Tyler was just shy of three years old, we went to the zoo. We were having a great time looking at the animals, and Tyler was especially excited to see the monkeys. But, as we stood near the monkeys' cage, Tyler's excitement suddenly turned into frustration. He really wanted the monkeys to pay attention to him, but they were busy doing their own monkey things. This made Tyler upset, and he started shouting at them and stomping his feet. The next thing I knew, he was climbing up on the railing, so I had to grab him quickly and roughly. That led to him emitting a loud wail, which in turn caused the monkeys to start their own loud chattering. Naturally, some wag in the newly formed audience suggested I let Tyler join his brothers in the cage. Then, one of the zoo attendants came to ask if the monkeys had flung feces at my child and if that was why he was upset.*

We left the zoo quickly, and Tyler screamed all the way back to the car. Once we drove off, he settled down and fell asleep.

Pretty much all toddlers have tantrums, though not all have meltdowns. In a tantrum, a child still has some self-control; in a meltdown, they continue acting out until they're exhausted, although comforting them sometimes works.What causes tantrums? Around the age of two and even three, children are at a crucial juncture of development where their language and emotional regulation skills are still maturing. This sets the stage for tantrums and meltdowns, as they grapple with their emotions in a world they're just beginning to understand.[3]

The frequency and intensity of tantrums also depend on the child's inborn temperament. Psychologists categorize children's temperaments as "high-reactive" or "low-reactive," and infants' temperaments can be identified by four months. The indicators are attentiveness, how readily they get distressed by certain events, how easy or hard it is to soothe them, and how often they cry.[4] Dr. Peterson identifies the following categories: (1) agreeable (these children want to please their parents and other people); (2) independent (want to what they want); (3) rule-oriented (prefer ordered and even strict environments); and (4) unpredictable (reject any order at all).[5]

Typical Tantrum Triggers

Frustration

We all get frustrated, but for toddlers, this feeling can be especially intense. There they are, trying to tell you what they want (and their want, remember, is *very* important), and these big fools can't understand or are refusing to obey.

Hunger and Fatigue

If a hungry man is an angry man, a hungry toddler is a berserker. Feed accordingly. Ditto with sleep.

Sensory Overload

If your toddler has sensory sensitivities, bright lights, loud noises, and unfamiliar textures can trigger them.

Seeking Attention

Toddlers crave attention, so if they feel you're paying too much attention to mommy or Monday Night Football, they might throw a tantrum just to regain focus on themselves.

Unmet Desires

Toddlers have a limited understanding of delayed gratification. When they can't have something they want immediately, like a toy or a treat, the resulting disappointment can escalate into a tantrum.

Emotional Expression

Toddlers are still learning to identify and manage their emotions. Sometimes, tantrums serve as a way for them to release pent-up feelings of anger, sadness, or even excitement.

The link between these tantrum triggers is your toddler's inability to understand their own emotions, especially anger. While anger is often viewed as a negative emotion, it is, in fact, essential to establishing your place in the social order and keeping that order stable. Anger is entwined with our sense of fairness, and children often throw tantrums because they feel they deserve or need something that is being deliberately withheld.

It's important to see our child's tantrums not as calculated misbehavior but as emotional turmoil that provides us with opportunities to hone their emotional intelligence. Always remember: temper tantrums are a normal part of a toddler's journey toward emotional maturity.

Once you instill that mindset in yourself, you can use some proven techniques to handle these inevitable outbursts effectively.

Toddler Tantrum Tips

By understanding and implementing appropriate strategies, you'll be able to defuse tantrums and foster healthy emotional development in your child. Use whichever of the following ten strategies you believe will work best for your child, depending on their temperament and the specific situation:

1. *Handle aggressive behavior immediately.* Address any aggressive behavior promptly. Calmly intervene if your child becomes physically aggressive, ensuring the safety of everyone involved.

2. *Don't yell.* Shouting at your child can escalate the situation. Maintain a calm tone to prevent further agitation.

3. *Let your child be angry.* The trick here is to let them express their anger, but show them how to do so in a controlled and respectful way. (I didn't say these tips would be easy.

4. *Pick your battles.* Not every situation warrants a showdown. Evaluate the importance of the issue at hand and decide if it's worth the conflict.

5. *Use brief commands.* Keep your instructions simple and clear. Too much information can overwhelm a frustrated child.

6. *Distract them.* Redirect their attention to something engaging. This technique often helps shift their focus away from the trigger of the tantrum.

7. *Give them a hug.* This can provide comfort, especially during a meltdown. Or it might make them even angrier. It's usually best to still hug them, but make sure not to restrict their movements since that may add to their frustration. If they hit you, let go.

8. *Help undo frustration.* If you can identify what triggered the tantrum, help them solve the problem. This does not mean giving in to their demands since that will only teach them that problems can be solved with tantrums.

9. *Stick to your demands.* If the tantrum is related to setting boundaries, remain firm in your decision. Consistency helps children understand limits.

10. *Laugh it off.* Use humor to lighten the mood. Sometimes, a funny face or a playful comment can dissolve tension. On the other hand, they may get even more angry if they feel you're laughing at them—remember, their problems are more important than the threat of nuclear war.[6]

Every child is unique, so it's important to adapt these techniques to your child's personality and preferences. By responding calmly, empathetically, and consistently, you can navigate tantrums and help your child learn to manage their emotions while maintaining a strong and trusting parent-child bond.

Teaching Toddlers to Teach Themselves

Managing your toddler's tantrums is only your short-term goal. What you really want is to help them manage their tantrums for themselves. This is the key to later emotional maturity, so you want them to gain this ability as early as possible. As Dr. Jordan Peterson argues in his book *Beyond Order*, "This must happen by the age of four, or it may never happen. A child must be sufficiently self-organizing to be desirable to his or her peers by the age of four or risk permanent ostracism."[7]

It's therefore crucial that you, as a dad, adopt this long-term perspective. When Ashley was two years old, she would often demand (loudly) items that we saw while at the supermarket—usually snacks, sometimes toys, occasionally broccoli (yes, she liked broccoli). To nip this in the bud, I told her she had to ask, not tell, me what she wanted, or else I would stop bringing her to the supermarket. I also explained that if something was too expensive, we would not buy it. After that, supermarket shopping with her became a pleasure because we would have conversations as we went through the aisles. She would ask nicely if she wanted something, and I could start teaching her both numbers and independence by having her check the price and get the item off the shelf.

Try using a range of techniques that consistently guide and nurture your child's emotional development. This paves the way for them to develop lasting self-control and emotional intelligence. The following approaches can help you achieve these outcomes:

- Support independent problem-solving.
- Consider timing for communication.
- Guide during emotional moments.
- Navigate the calm-down phase.
- Teach healthy coping mechanisms.[8]

When your youngster becomes upset, it's crucial to provide them with proper guidance. For example, if they're using building blocks and their structure falls over, let them fix it themselves, even—or especially—if you see they're getting frustrated. With consistent practice, they will come to realize that they can calm down and find solutions. Allowing them to experience challenges fosters resilience and hones their ability to devise solutions. This kind of empowerment can reduce the frequency and intensity of tantrums as they learn to navigate their emotions more effectively.

Attempting to reason with your child during a tantrum is an exercise in futility. You can't reason with a child screaming, "I want, I want, I want...!" Besides, well-intentioned remarks can make them even angrier. It's more effective to let them learn how to calm down at their own rate. So, just comfort them and wait for them to settle down. Then you can talk to them about what just happened.

If your child is causing a disturbance in a public setting, it's advisable to take them to a private area to cool off. Toddlers act out to gain attention, so withholding that additional spotlight can expedite the dissipation of their tantrums. Remember, avoid punishing them for it, but don't give in, either.

When they're in the process of calming down, be present with them, but minimize eye contact and talk. Allow them the space to work through their emotions. The objective is for them to regain control in a few seconds. It is acceptable if they're venting or having an outburst, provided they eventually calm down. During this period, give your child some space. This reinforces the core message that tantrums don't get your toddler the attention they are seeking. (If they hit or throw things, then, of course, you must intervene.) This approach teaches them healthier ways to manage emotions and navigate challenges without relying on outbursts.

While they're in the "calm down" phase, make sure they see you being calm, composed, and collected. You can even initiate an activity they enjoy, like playing with a favorite toy or enjoying a snack. After they've settled, you can share in the activity or treat. Once they've fully calmed down, offering a hug and commendation for handling the situation is an effective way to close the incident. Teach them to express their feelings through words rather than through tantrums. This helps them develop emotional intelligence and effective communication skills.

This process is aimed at teaching them self-control, a skill they'll hopefully carry with them throughout life. Each child is unique, so what resonates with one might not suit another.

Help your toddler practice techniques such as deep breathing, counting, or using stress-relieving objects like fidget spinners or whatever helps focus their attention. Explain how they must do these exercises whenever they start to feel upset or angry. These strategies empower them to manage frustration and anger constructively.

It's also important to acknowledge and reward good behavior, offering positive attention when they're behaving well. This reinforces self-control and encourages them to continue making positive choices. If you're going out, especially for several hours, ensure your toddler is well-rested, well-fed, and comfortable.

Setting clear boundaries and expectations consistently helps your child understand what is acceptable behavior. Remember, do not punish tantrums, but do not give in to them, either.

Finally, always show how to remain calm, even in frustrating situations. Your composure, especially as a dad, sets a positive example for your child to follow.

Creating an Anti-Tantrum Space

Tantrums are caused by a combination of a toddler's temperament, immediate situation, and the environment in which they are nurtured. We have no control over the first and only limited control over the second, but we can create an environment that teaches our child to cope with the first two factors. Here's a list of how to do this:

1. *Provide emotional support.* This is the foundation of a child's self-confidence. By giving your child love,

attention, and respect as a dad, you create a safe space where your toddler feels understood and valued. This empowers them to explore their interests and abilities without fear of judgment.

2. *Enable rich sensory experiences.* Children are naturally curious and learn through their senses. Providing a variety of sensory experiences—such as tactile, auditory, visual, and olfactory stimuli—fuels their cognitive and creative development. Activities that involve exploring textures, listening to different sounds, and engaging with various scents stimulate their senses and foster cognitive connections.

3. *Create spaces within the house for different activities.* Dedicating specific areas within the home for play, reading, art, and relaxation helps your child to pursue their interests independently. These spaces also allow for focused engagement without distractions, fostering concentration and a sense of ownership.

4. *Provide a variety of educational toys and books.* A diverse array of educational toys, books, and materials stimulates children's intellectual growth. Toys that encourage problem-solving, creativity, and critical thinking, along with a wide selection of age-appropriate books, expose children to new ideas and concepts. These resources support their cognitive development and ignite a lifelong love for learning.

5. *Establish a daily structured routine.* A structured routine can provide children with a sense of stability and predictability. Consistent meal times, playtime, learning activities, and rest periods may contribute to a child's overall well-being. However, these outcomes depend really on your child's inborn temperament and personality. Adapt accordingly.

6. *Use complex language.* Language is a powerful tool for cognitive development and communication. Engaging children in conversations, reading stories aloud, and introducing new vocabulary enhances their language skills. Once you do this, the phrase "use your words" can become an effective short-circuit to tantrums.

7. *Be present and engage with your child.* One of the most impactful ways to foster a thriving environment is by being fully present and engaged with your child. Actively participate in their play, discussions, and activities.[9]

Creating this kind of home environment empowers children to explore, learn, and develop into capable individuals who are well-equipped to navigate the world around them.

KEY TAKEAWAYS

- Tantrums are a natural part of toddlers' development.
- You need to teach them how to manage their emotions, preferably before they reach four years of age.
- Children can attain self-control with the right guidance and support.

Once you've taught your toddler how to handle their tantrums, you'll feel like you can handle any challenge they throw at you. Now, though, you have to face the battle for bedtime. The nightmare begins.

4

SOLVING SLEEP WOES

Before we became parents, we all knew how to put children to sleep. We imagined we would sit at the side of their beds and read them a bedtime story, and they would drift off peacefully. We would finish reading, tuck them in, and they would go to sleep.

That's how it happened on TV, after all. Then, when we actually became parents, we realized that TV was absolute and unadulterated BS (pardon my abbreviation). Now, we have discovered real children fight sleep. They do it as infants, and they do it even more when they become toddlers. If they even listen to the story we're reading, they'll interrupt with all sorts of questions, not because they're interested, but just to stay awake for longer. If we even try to leave the room while they're still awake, they'll beg for another story (or, worse, ask you to read over the same one). If you refuse and leave the room, with the laughable instruction, "Close your eyes and go to sleep," it won't be five minutes before you hear the call from the bedroom, "Daddy, I want some water."

When I was first trying to get my three-year-old son, Tyler, to stick to a sleep routine, pretty much nothing worked. At first, I tried tiring him out during the day by taking him to the park or playing games with him. However, that only seemed to make him more hyperactive and less likely to sleep at night. I tried reading him a story, giving him a warm bath, and then putting him to bed at the same time every night. But he would resist going to bed, even getting angry or crying. I even tried bribing him with treats or toys if he went to bed on time. That only worked for a few nights before he started resisting again.

So, I started reading up on toddler sleep, and in this chapter, I'll share with you what worked for me and what may work for your child (because all children are different and, in the final analysis, we parents know more than any expert what's best for our child and our family.)

That said, getting our toddlers to follow a sleep routine is probably the hardest challenge we have as parents— harder than stopping their temper tantrums, harder than potty training (next chapter), harder than explaining where they came from (not included in this book). It also seems to be harder for American parents than parents anywhere else in the world, which suggests we may be doing something wrong. (Yes, I know that's a hard concept for us to grasp.)

In my previous book for first-time Dads, I mentioned America is just about the only society on earth where parents believe that not only should parents sleep in a separate bed but in a separate room as well. That belief arises out of the American ethos of independence (we think that putting our babies in their own room fosters self-reliance), our busy routines (time spent getting our children to sleep means less sleep time for us), and simply the luxury of having enough space to accomplish this.

Biologically, however, babies don't enjoy being alone. Why would they? Any baby who, in prehistoric times, remained calm when alone would have been more likely to be snatched by predators since they wouldn't have sounded an alarm (i.e., cried hysterically) if any strange creature approached. Such infants would never have grown up and passed on their calm genes.

Here's what I want you to keep in mind as you go through this chapter: contrary to what you'll read in most parenting books, getting our toddlers to follow a regular sleep schedule is more for our benefit than theirs. As Jim McKenna, an infant development expert, states, "It's never the sleeping arrangements that decide how a child will turn out; it's the overall nature of the child's relationship with the parents."[1]

SLEEP BASICS EVERY DAD SHOULD KNOW

When kids are between one and two years old, they usually need about 11 to 14 hours of sleep each day, including naps. But as they grow, their sleep patterns change. At around 18 months, most toddlers switch from having two naps to just one afternoon nap. So, if your toddler doesn't want to nap in the morning, they might be ready for an afternoon nap instead.

"Once babies become toddlers, they may start waking up at night," writes journalist Christine Gross-Loh in her book *Parenting Without Borders*. "This toddler night-waking happens to most kids, peaking between one-and-a-half to two years, when they get their two-year molars."[2]

They may also wake up to make sure their parents are close by. Studies show that co-sleeping children experience more frequent but shorter night-wakings than children who sleep alone.[3]

They wake up if the temperature in their room is uncomfortable. Tyler used to push off the covers at night, so in the colder months, we used to dress him in thick pajamas before putting him to sleep. Although he would sleep through a thunderstorm, Ashley used to wake up if we had to turn the TV on too loud. (I quickly learned to use captions.)

We dads thrive on finding ways to protect our families. These safety precautions may come as second nature to you! Here are some of the basic precautions we need to put in place when our children become toddlers:

- *Strings and cords*: Get rid of any items with ties, strings, or cords in your toddler's crib or within their reach. All of these pose a danger of strangling. Ditto for curtains, window blind cords, and any decorations that your toddler might grab.
- *Climbing out of the crib*: Some toddlers may attempt to climb over the crib railing just to see if they can. To stop this, limit the number of toys within their reach, as they might use them as makeshift stepping stones. And don't use crib bumper pads, which your toddler will find a convenient step to use for climbing.
- *Adjusting the crib mattress*: Put the crib mattress at its lowest level. This can help prevent your toddler from gaining enough height to climb out. If your child continues to attempt crib escapes, however, you might transition them to a toddler bed or a "big kid" bed equipped with a side rail and start reading up on careers in security for when they go to college.
- *Safety gates*: Installing a safety gate in the doorway of your child's room stops them from wandering around the house unattended, especially if they escape their crib.
- *Furniture safety*: Besides crib safety, it's essential to secure other furniture items in your child's room.

Use furniture straps to prevent bookshelves, dressers, or other tall pieces from tipping over. Toddlers are naturally curious and may attempt to climb on furniture, making it crucial to anchor these items securely.

- *Socket covers and childproofing*: Childproofing your toddler's room is crucial. Cover electrical sockets with socket covers, secure cords out of reach, and ensure furniture corners are protected with bumpers to prevent injury in case of falls.
- *Secure heavy objects*: Keep heavy objects like TVs or mirrors securely fastened to the wall to prevent accidents caused by tipping.[4]

Remember that toddler safety needs evolve as your child grows and becomes more mobile. Regularly reassess their environment for potential hazards and make adjustments to ensure they don't get injured.

SLEEP ROUTINES ARE NEVER ROUTINE

For many toddlers, having a routine before bedtime helps them sleep better. But, as I keep saying, you need to figure out what's best for your child. If their temperament inclines them towards structure and order, then a bedtime routine will do them a world of good. Even your cultural environment affects how you create a bedtime routine (or don't). In the US, for example, some cultures pay less attention to putting children to sleep. In other countries like India or Argentina, routines can also be different, with children either allowed to stay up when they get tired or sleep whenever they want.

A bedtime routine means doing the same things before your toddler goes to sleep. This routine can take place about an hour before they turn off the lights and actually fall asleep. It's not about things they do while falling asleep, like being rocked or fed. These routines help kids know it's time to sleep.

Activities may include:

- *Bath time:* A warm bath can be a soothing and enjoyable activity before bed.
- *Pajama time:* Let your toddler pick out their pajamas, promoting a sense of autonomy.
- *Story time:* Reading a bedtime story is a classic way to wind down before sleep.
- *Cuddle time:* Cuddling and talking with your toddler in bed.
- *Lullabies or soft music.* Play soft and soothing lullabies or calming music in the background.
- *Dimming the lights:* As bedtime approaches, gradually dim the lights in the room to signal to your toddler that it's time to wind down and sleep.[5]

Creating a bedtime routine is about making a plan to help your toddler sleep better. Even though routines can be different, the important thing is to do things that help your toddler feel relaxed and ready for sleep. This routine can change as your toddler grows.

Once you've found the right combination, like a warm bath and a bedtime story, stick with it. Decide how many drinks of water you'll allow while they're going to sleep and how many times you'll retrieve the toy that's thrown out of the crib in defiance of bedtime. Get your toddler used to the rules and stick to them. This not only helps your child get more sleep now but also helps you later if other, more serious discipline problems arise.

If your toddler wakes in the middle of the night, you'll still want to quietly and quickly provide reassurance that everything is okay and you are close by. But too much interaction can backfire, so keep your nighttime "visits" brief and boring for your toddler.

If your child is an early riser, help keep sunlight from waking them by keeping curtains or blinds closed. Also, try putting a few safe toys in the crib to keep them busy in the morning (to avoid them keeping you busy).

What to Do and What Not to Do

In establishing a bedtime routine, keep your core goal in mind: to create a consistent and calming routine that sets the stage for a peaceful night's rest. Here are some *do's and don'ts* that I found useful with my children:

Do:

1. *Establish a bedtime routine early.* Start the routine while they're still young. This helps them learn healthy sleep habits from an early age.
2. *Be consistent.* Toddlers thrive on routine, so try to do the same things in the same order each night. This helps them know what to expect, making it easier for them to wind down.
3. *Include dental hygiene.* Brushing teeth is a healthy habit to include in the routine. It signals that it's almost time for bed and keeps their little teeth healthy.
4. *Keep it short.* Toddlers have short attention spans, so keep the routine around 20-30 minutes. This prevents them from getting overtired and makes the routine manageable.
5. *Make it appropriate.* Choose activities that suit your toddler's age and temperament. Just because they're two doesn't mean a book or song for two-year-olds will hold their attention. Let them decide what's interesting by offering a variety.
6. *Have them use the potty.* Encourage them to use the potty before bed. This reduces the chances of nighttime bathroom trips, helping them sleep more soundly.
7. *Prepare for a little crying.* Sometimes, toddlers cry when it's time for bed. It's okay to comfort them, but also let them learn to self-soothe a bit.

8. *Use a security object.* A favorite stuffed animal or blanket can provide comfort and a sense of security, making it easier for them to fall asleep.

Don't:

1. *Allow stimulating activities before bed.* Avoid energetic play or screen time close to bedtime. These activities can make it hard for them to settle down.
2. *Think bad sleep habits will just go away.* Address sleep issues early. If they're struggling to sleep through the night, it's better to make changes sooner rather than later.
3. *Create counter-productive sleep associations.* Be careful with associations like rocking them to sleep. If they get used to falling asleep in a certain way, they might have trouble when things change.
4. *Drag it out.* Keep the routine focused and avoid prolonging it. Lingering too long might make them overtired and cranky.[6]

IF YOUR TODDLER ISN'T A ROUTINE FOLLOWER

If these techniques don't work, get more sophisticated. This will require more work on your part, but if you can get them to sleep at regular hours, it'll be worth it. So, you can try creating a personalized book with photos or illustrations depicting a typical day in your child's life—

including their bedtime routine steps. Read this book to them regularly, both before bedtime and during the day. This will—hopefully!—help them understand what's expected of them when it's time for bed.

Another tactic you can use is called "Twinkle Interruptus." This method is for toddlers who want you to stay with them until they fall asleep: As you're about to give good-night kisses, suddenly say, "Oh dear! Hold on! Just a moment! I need to check something! I'll be back shortly!" Step out of the room for a few seconds before returning. When you come back, praise them for waiting patiently. Continue with the bedtime routine and, once again, find a reason to leave ("Oops! I must use the bathroom! Give your favorite toy a hug, and I'll be back very quickly!"). Repeat this a few times, gradually extending the time your little one waits. Over several nights, you'll likely discover that your toddler has fallen asleep while awaiting your return!

If, after you leave, your child wakes up and comes to find you or tells you to come back and put them to sleep, try a strategy called "special passes." These can be paper cut-outs or poker chips, which you leave near their bed. Tell them that, at bedtime, they can use these special passes to get you to come back for water, an extra kiss, or anything else—each act costing them one pass. You can also offer them a prize; if they still have a pass in the morning, they can exchange it for a special reward, such as a temporary tattoo or a chocolate or whatever small thing they like. If they have two passes, they get an even bigger prize, like an extra ten minutes after the usual bedtime. This method works best with older toddlers.[7]

Don't hesitate to make any adjustments you believe will make the bedtime routine easier. For instance, if you think your toddler may go to bed too early, try pushing their bedtime routine 15 minutes later for two to three nights. If you think the bedtime is too late, start the routine 15 minutes earlier every two to three nights. Either approach should work within a week or two.

DON'T FORGET YOU NEED SLEEP, TOO!

If your toddler is two years old, that probably means you've been sleep-deprived for two years. The biggest benefit of getting them to sleep at regular times is that it allows you to finally catch up on your sleep. Once you've gotten your toddler into their routine, you may actually find it hard to get a full night's sleep because you've become so accustomed to doing without.

So, here are some tips for parents to get a good night's sleep:

1. *Have an early dinner.* Eating a heavy meal too close to bedtime can cause discomfort and indigestion, making it difficult to fall asleep. Try to have dinner at least two to three hours before bedtime.

2. *Exercise regularly.* Regular exercise can help you fall asleep faster and enjoy deeper sleep. However, avoid exercising too close to bedtime since this can make you feel more alert and awake.

3. *Take time to relax.* Engage in relaxing activities such as reading, taking a warm bath, or getting a massage from your partner.

4. *Establish a set bedtime.* Going to bed and waking up at the same time every day can help regulate your body's internal clock and improve the quality of your sleep.

5. *Follow a bedtime routine.* Establishing a relaxing bedtime routine can signal your body that it's time to sleep. Consider activities such as taking a warm bath, reading a book, or listening to calming music.

6. *Maintain a comfortable temperature in the bedroom.* A cool room temperature of around 65°F (18°C) is ideal for most people to sleep comfortably.

7. *Sensory deprivation.* Use earplugs or white noise machines to block out external noise that may disturb your sleep. Also, wear a sleep mask.

8. *Don't go to bed angry.* Avoid engaging in arguments or stressful conversations before bedtime, as they can make it difficult to fall asleep. It's also good for your relationship.

9. *Get sunlight in the morning.* Exposure to natural sunlight in the morning can help regulate your

body's internal clock and improve your sleep quality.

10. *Take naps.* Taking naps earlier in the day can help you feel more alert during the day without interfering with your nighttime sleep.[8]

KEY TAKEAWAYS

- A regular bedtime routine makes everybody rested.
- Use whatever combination of techniques works for your toddler.
- Make sure you get enough sleep, too.

In the next chapter, I address the subject that parents typically dread the most: potty training. Reader, beware, you're about to read a lot of crap.

A Powerful Gift You Can Give Other Toddler Dads

"The fundamental job of a toddler is to rule the universe."

— *LAWERENCE KUTNER*

If you were one of those dads who reads everything about becoming a father and then quickly realized that the newborn stage is over as soon as you've figured out how to get almost enough sleep, you're certainly not the only one.

We all want to be the best dads we can be, and when we hear that our first child is on the way, many of us do everything we can to prepare. We learn about pregnancy, how to baby-proof the house, and read up on feeding and sleeping routines. But all those new baby books only take you so far ... and suddenly, you have a toddler on your hands, and the whole game changes.

That's why you're here, and it's because I've been there too that I wrote this book.

I'm not saying there aren't plenty of books about toddlers out there, but so many of them miss the specific guidance fathers need ... because our role is different to Mom's, and we want to make sure they get the best of both worlds.

I know how daunting it is when you suddenly realize you have a toddler on your hands, and now that you do, too, I'm hoping you'll help me reassure more dads like us.

By leaving a review of this book on Amazon, you'll help take the mystery out of the toddler years for other fathers and make sure they find the guidance they're looking for.

Every review is a road sign pointing readers in the direction of the specific information they're seeking, and your review will help countless dads ace the toddler game.

Thank you so much for your support. All of us want to do the best we can as fathers, and when we help each other out, we have even more chance of being the dads we really want to be.

Scan the QR code here

5

POTTY TRAINING LIKE A PRO

When my children were still infants, nothing bonded me more closely to them as a dad than bottle-feeding. When they became toddlers, I got the same feeling from wiping their bums.

Yes, I know it sounds strange, but it makes sense—after all, in both situations, we are performing the most basic tasks for another little person. By the same token, we measure their growing up by their ability to feed and clean themselves.

Rest assured, the latter will come. It seems hard to conceive when your toddler is still in diapers, but they will not only learn to use the toilet but also wipe themselves quite clean. Potty training should speed up this process.

In this chapter, we'll explore how to prepare your child for this milestone, implement a step-by-step training guide that eases both of you into the process, and we'll discover creative ways to celebrate progress so the lessons stick.

IS YOUR TODDLER READY FOR THE POTTY?

In America, most toddlers aren't fully potty trained until they're past three years of age. In China, most toddlers are fully potty trained before they're 18 months old.[1]

There's no difference between the bowels of American and Chinese children. The difference lies in cultural expectations and, more importantly, disposable diapers. The first disposable diapers were invented in the 1940s, but really started selling in the 1970s.[2] Before that, American children were usually toilet-trained by 18 months, just like the Chinese. What this means is that, yes, you can potty train your toddler at or before two, but it will require effort and a readiness to clean up their accidents. So, if your floors have carpet instead of tiles or hardwood, be prepared to roll up the rugs (and your sleeves) if you're taking this route.

Determining whether your child is ready for toilet training can vary from one child to another. Five typical indicators are:

1. *Showing interest in the potty*: They ask questions or make comments about the toilet or potty chair.
2. *Staying dry for longer periods*: They stay dry for at least a couple of hours at a time and wake up from naps with a dry diaper. This shows they're developing bladder control, which is a crucial aspect of potty-training readiness.
3. *Communicating the need to go*: They communicate when they have to go, either through words, gestures, or facial expressions. They might say "potty" or use other words to let you know they need to use the bathroom.
4. *Showing discomfort with dirty diapers*: They display discomfort or displeasure when their diaper is soiled or wet. This shows that they're noticing their bodily sensations, which is a crucial step towards potty training.
5. *Showing independence*: They say "no" to diaper changes, want to dress or undress themselves, or display interest in wearing underwear like older children.[3]

Once you see all or some of these signs, begin toilet training. Let your toddler proceed at their own pace, keeping spare clothing on hand. Also, load up on cleaning supplies, especially paper towels, for wiping up the floor.

One item I found useful was disposable training pants. These pants pull up and down easily, making it more manageable for toddlers to use public restrooms or portable potties while outside the comfort of home.

The pants solved the discrepancy between daytime and nighttime control for both Ashley and Tyler. While some toddlers might have a firm grasp on their bladder and bowel functions during the day, nighttime can be a different story. Training pants provided an extra layer of protection during nighttime slumber, allowing for a more comfortable night's sleep and, for us parents, fewer messy sheets.

The training pants also came in handy when we were on the move, whether on a trip to the park, a visit to the grocery store, or a long car ride. My advice is to use them until your child consistently keeps them dry for a few days, signaling readiness for underwear.

The one drawback is that using disposable training pants might inadvertently signal to children that it's acceptable to use them like diapers, hence slowing down the toilet-teaching process. So, keep an eye out for any such regression as you potty train. Ultimately, every child is unique, and the decision to use training pants should be based on your child's specific needs and readiness. You will know best.

POTTY TRAINING HELPS YOUR TODDLER AND YOU

Potty training is a big deal. It can be daunting and intimidating. But do not worry, I have tons of personal experience that I would love to share with you. Here are five key benefits to potty training—and the earlier you do it, the greater the benefits.

1. *Sense of accomplishment and independence*: Perhaps one of the most important benefits is the sense of accomplishment and independence it instills in children. Learning to use the toilet on their own gives them a newfound sense of control over their bodies and actions. It's a source of pride for them to achieve this level of self-sufficiency.
2. *Financial savings*: Potty training also translates into financial savings for parents. Bid farewell to the recurring expenses of diapers and welcome the freedom from constantly restocking them. This shift can provide a welcome relief to the family budget.
3. *Reduced exposure to harsh chemicals*: For parents who have used disposable diapers, potty training brings an added health benefit. It puts an end to prolonged exposure to chemicals like dioxins, which are present in some disposable diapers. These aren't likely to affect your child in any significant way, but if it's a worry you have, you

may want to start potty training very early or even bypass diapers altogether by trying elimination training instead (which I dealt with in the last section of this chapter).

4. *Enhanced confidence*: As children master the entire process of using the toilet, including wiping or washing themselves and their hands, their confidence soars. This newfound confidence extends beyond the bathroom and empowers them to take on more complex challenges in other aspects of life.

5. *Time and energy savings*: Last but not least, potty training is a time-and-energy saver for parents and caregivers. No more changing diapers, dealing with diaper bags, or endless trips to the changing table. It streamlines daily routines and allows parents to focus their time and energy on other important aspects of parenting (such as making another baby or at least having fun pretending to try).

While guiding your child through this process, a gentle approach is paramount. Let them take charge instead of imposing strict expectations. At the same time, excessive leniency might lead to delays in toilet training. I am including some warnings below, for information only, because with even minimal guidance, most three-year-olds potty train readily.

- Daytime accidents with urine and stool
- Increased susceptibility to urinary tract infections
- Bedwetting during naps or nighttime
- Loss of control over bowel movements

Involve everyone with potty training. If your child attends daycare, engage the caregivers and request their cooperation in reinforcing your efforts. Be patient and understanding when accidents occur with pee or poop in training pants or diapers—never scold your toddler. This will only delay them becoming toilet-trained. You should also maintain a consistent routine to establish a sense of predictability. Don't force the training, though. If your child displays anxiety, reassure them and take brief breaks. It's also useful to celebrate every achievement. Praise each successful trip to the potty, changing clothes for themselves, hand washing, and so on.[4]

You also need to make your toddler conscious of their bowels and bladders. Children naturally become engrossed in their play or activities and may not always remember to ask to use the toilet. To avoid accidents, remind them at regular intervals if they need to pee or poop. Even if they decline, these reminders can help them stay aware of their bodily cues and the importance of timely bathroom breaks. If you have trouble remembering, set a poop alarm on your smartphone like I did. (Just don't call it "Time to Poop" like I did because people who saw it going off gave me strange looks.)

When your toddler goes, remind them to wipe the toilet seat before use, flush the toilet after, and always wash their hands thoroughly. Teaching these habits alongside potty training ensures a well-rounded approach to personal hygiene.

TIPS FOR MAKING POTTY TRAINING ENJOYABLE

Making potty training a delightful adventure can make the journey smoother for your toddler and less of a chore for you. Here are some creative ways to make potty training an enjoyable experience:

1. *Special shopping trip*: Kick off the potty-training journey with a special shopping trip. Take your child to choose essential potty items like a potty chair and training pants. Let them select products adorned with their favorite characters, granting them a sense of ownership in this process. Make it all about potty training to make them feel proud of this exciting step.

2. *Potty training scavenger hunt*: Transform potty training into an engaging scavenger hunt. After acquiring potty essentials, create a game where your child hunts for their training pants, potty chair, toilet paper, and soap around the house. This interactive activity not only makes learning

fun but also reinforces the importance of these items.

3. *Creative sticker chart*: Make potty training visually rewarding by designing a sticker chart. You can either print a pre-made one or create a customized chart together. Gather supplies like poster board, stickers, and markers, and let your child decorate. The chart serves as a fun way to track progress and celebrate achievements.

4. *Unique "Going Potty" song*: Get creative by crafting a unique "going potty" song together. Adapt your child's favorite song with potty-related lyrics and sing it during potty sessions. This musical addition makes potty time something to look forward to and helps them stay patient while sitting on the potty.

5. *Potty time story time*: Dedicate special books exclusively for potty time. Choose silly kids' poetry, brightly illustrated picture books, or those with funny words and rhythms. Reading together while waiting on the potty not only entertains but also creates anticipation for potty breaks.

6. *Potty training science experiment*: Turn potty time into a science experiment by adding drops of food coloring to the toilet water. Encourage your child to guess the resulting color when they pee, introducing an element of fun and curiosity.

7. *Potty training treasure chest*: Create a treasure chest for potty training rewards. Start with a shoebox or

plastic container, and let your child decorate it. Fill it with small toys, books, or rewards for accomplishing potty-related tasks. This personalized approach adds excitement and motivation.

Incorporating these activities into potty training not only simplifies the process but also fosters a sense of accomplishment and excitement on this journey to independence.[5]

ELIMINATING THE DIAPER

Elimination Communication (EC), also known as natural infant hygiene, is an alternative approach to traditional potty training. Unlike the conventional method, where children transition from diapers to using a potty, EC focuses on early communication between parents or caregivers and infants to address their elimination needs. This practice is rooted in observing and responding to a baby's cues, allowing them to signal when they need to eliminate waste. While it may not be a mainstream choice, it has gained popularity among parents seeking a diaper-free or eco-friendly approach to infant hygiene.

EC hinges on understanding and responding to a baby's cues and signals for elimination. According to writer Mei-Ling Hopgood in her book *How Eskimos Keep Their Babies Warm*, "The key...is being relaxed about nudity, body waste, and accidents."[6]

How EC Works

Timing

Babies often exhibit predictable patterns for elimination. Some may pee upon waking from naps or nighttime sleep, while others may need to go shortly after eating. Keeping a log of your baby's potty times can help discern their unique schedule. Alternatively, you can establish regular intervals throughout the day when you visit the toilet together.

Signals

Babies are adept at conveying their need to eliminate in various ways. They may cry, fuss, become still, or pause from activities. Squirming or waking from sleep can also be indicative. Each baby's signals are unique but typically consistent. Over time, some babies may even seek their designated potty spot when they need to go.

Intuition

As a dad, you may develop an intuitive sense of when your baby needs to go. This deep understanding can evolve with time, allowing you to anticipate their needs, even without visual cues.

Cues

Cueing is communication between parent and baby during EC. You can use a specific sound, like "shhh" or "sss" each time your baby urinates. After a while, they may associate this sound with going to the bathroom, making it a useful tool for encouraging them to pee. You can also employ particular positions or holds to signal toileting time. These actions and sounds become a language that your baby can comprehend, and they may even start using some of these cues themselves to show when it's time to go.

EC requires keen observation, patience, and a deep connection with your child. It's based on the premise that babies are born with a natural instinct to communicate their elimination needs. Benefits of EC include using fewer or no diapers, making it an eco-friendly option that contributes to less waste. It may also help promote early awareness of bodily functions in babies, potentially leading to earlier independence in toileting. But, make no mistake, the EC approach requires lots of time and attention and, depending on your toddler, many clean-ups in Aisle 7. (I mean that literally because it happened to my friend Roger.)

When and How to Start

Once you understand the basics, you then need to decide how and when you'll start. Some parents choose full-time

EC soon after birth. Others approach it with more compromise. This is considered part-time.[7]

It can mean anything from only using a toilet after feeding and doing diapers during naps and nights to always using a toilet at home and diapers while out. Alternatively, you may choose to use the toilet just once before bed each night.

Here are some items you'll need for EC:

- *Potty chair:* Invest in a potty chair like the Baby Bjorn Potty, recommended for its small size and versatile insert. It's ideal for both tiny infants and older ones. For those on a budget, a sink or small plastic container can serve as a makeshift potty receptacle.
- *Clothing:* Opt for crotchless or easily removable clothing items to facilitate swift transitions during potty moments. Consider stocking up on practical items like baby leg warmers and nightgowns designed to open at the bottom, ensuring accessibility.
- *Backup diapers:* While the goal is to reduce diaper reliance, having backup diapers on hand is sensible. Choose cloth diapers, which may help babies become more attuned to wetness, or explore cloth underwear designed for infants, providing an eco-friendly and comfortable alternative.

EC is hailed by its proponents for delivering a multitude of advantages, both for parents and babies. These include:

- *Healthy skin:* EC might lead to a reduction in diaper rashes and other infections, like urinary tract infections. Although scientific research on this specific aspect of EC is limited, it stands to reason that when babies are not exposed to their waste for extended periods, their skin remains dry and healthier.
- *Waste reduction:* Regardless of whether you opt for full-time or part-time EC, parents use fewer diapers, resulting in a decrease in waste production. This diminished reliance on diapers aligns with a more eco-conscious approach, contributing to less waste in landfills and reduced water and energy consumption, even for those employing cloth diapers.
- *Financial savings:* By requiring fewer diapers, parents also save money on disposables and associated supplies. This not only eases the financial strain but also promotes a cost-effective and environmentally responsible lifestyle.
- *Enhanced comprehension:* Babies communicate through crying, and the need to eliminate is a significant cause of fussiness. By attuning themselves to their baby's cues, parents gain a better understanding of their infant's needs,

fostering greater empathy for their cries and promoting more effective caregiving.[8]

As Hopgood states, "It's not a task or a goal but simply something that is done with gentle patience and persistence." That's good advice for both EC and standard potty training.

KEY TAKEAWAYS

- Potty training is your toddler's first step towards independence.
- Don't set strict timeframes—your child will learn how to go.
- Patience and controlling your disgust reflex will make this task easier.

Cleaning your toddler's bottom is a no-boundary act, but once they've passed that stage, then setting boundaries is a useful method for establishing a healthy relationship now and in the future. The following chapter explains why and how.

6

RAISING A FREE SPIRIT WITHIN
SAFE BOUNDARIES

W hen our children were babies and crying at 3 a.m., we often wished for boundaries—preferably a nice thick soundproof wall. But we had made the little buggers and were now their slaves. Lack of sleep and sex notwithstanding, we thought it was a good deal.

Now, though, they're toddlers, and even though we still love them unconditionally, we must start setting boundaries for them. Contrary to what many parents nowadays seem to believe, boundaries are an essential part of responsible parenting, *especially* when it comes to toddlers.[1] We do our children no favors by letting them have their way at all times, in the mistaken notion that setting rules and restrictions will somehow hamper their development, creativity, or wonderful personalities. As the term 'snowflake' suggests (whether rightly or wrongly), it is precisely because parents indulged and protected their children too much that young people in college seem to lack resilience, let alone the mental toughness that is necessary to face life's inevitable challenges. Or maybe that is just my opinion, you can decide for yourself I suppose.Boundaries should begin with toddlers because, at that age, children are exploring the world around them and testing their limits. As a parent, it's your job to provide them with the guidance and structure they need to become self-reliant and independent adults.

While it may seem like your toddler is constantly pushing against your rules and boundaries, this is a normal and necessary part of their development. By testing limits, children learn what is acceptable behavior and what is not. They also learn about consequences and how their actions can impact others. Remember Jordan Peterson's Rule#5 from *12 Rules for Life*: "Don't let your children do anything that makes you dislike them." If you do, then other people will dislike them even more.

I also want to remind you of the following categories of child temperaments listed by Dr. Peterson: (1) agreeable (children who want to please their parents and other people); (2) independent (children who want what they want); (3) rule-oriented (prefer ordered and even strict environments); and (4) unpredictable (children who reject any order at all).[2]

As with the tantrums issue we discussed in chapter three, decide which category best fits your child. If they belong to (1) or (3), then setting boundaries will not only be a breeze but even unnecessary. If they're more in categories (2) and (4), then setting boundaries will be both more important and much harder, perhaps even requiring you to seek professional help.

So, let me repeat my mantra: *You*, as a dad, are the *expert* on your child. Even if you consult the child experts, take everything they say with a grain, if not a pound, of salt and adapt their advice to your child and your situation as you see fit. That also goes for the guidance I'm providing in this chapter and this book.

Toddlers are still developing their self-control and understanding of the world. Be patient with them as they learn and make mistakes. Instead of reacting with frustration, use challenging situations as opportunities for teaching and growth.

That said, let's examine how boundaries work and the best ways to apply them.

A BRIEF GUIDE TO BOUNDARIES

It's important to remember that while limits help children feel safe, they also need the freedom to try things out, make mistakes, and develop their independence. This is where boundaries come in. By setting clear boundaries, you can provide your child with the structure they need while still allowing them the freedom to explore and learn.

Chase Hill, Life Coach, states, "The idea is to allow a child to explore rules and boundaries so that they learn about limits and what happens when they're crossed."[3]

Boundaries also help children learn how to set limits for themselves and develop self-discipline. By learning to respect the boundaries you set for them, they will hopefully learn how to set their own boundaries and make good decisions on their own.

How do you establish and maintain these boundaries effectively? As with tantrums and potty training, everything starts with effective communication. For boundaries, that means using appropriate language to explain rules and expectations—and "appropriate" will depend on your child's vocabulary and level of comprehension. You should keep instructions concise and straightforward, use simple language, and avoid overwhelming them with lengthy explanations.

An especially useful approach is to develop a set of family rules that are simple, easy to understand, and applicable to various situations. If your toddler is capable and wants to, involve them in creating these rules. That gives them a sense of ownership and responsibility, which makes the rules easier to enforce.

You also must let your toddler know that it's okay to express their feelings and thoughts, including anger. "A child expressing anger should be allowed to explain how they feel," Hill writes. "But if they throw something in a rage or become physically violent, there has to be a consequence."[4]

This is the part that, as a dad, you may find most difficult. But, often, it's worse to set a boundary and not enforce it than to have no boundary at all. When you cannot follow through, your child may not take the rules seriously, leading to confusion and a lack of respect for boundaries.

Here are some guidelines to help you navigate this process, ensuring both you and your child benefit from clear and well-defined limits:

1. *Know your child's developmental stage.* Every child is unique and develops at their own pace. While age can serve as a rough guideline, it's essential that you identify the specific developmental stage your child is in. Setting boundaries that align with their abilities and understanding will be more effective —what works for a four-year-old, who recognizes that other people respond to how they behave, will not work for your egomaniacal two-year-old, who sees no connection between their actions and consequences. Not all children of the same age will have the same level of comprehension or self-control.

2. *Be consistent.* Children thrive on consistency. So, establish clear and simple rules that are easy to remember and enforce. You will almost certainly have to repeat a few times (well, maybe more than a few) because children's memories of rules are not always reliable, especially for stuff they don't *want* to remember. Ensure that your child fully understands what is expected of them and the consequences of breaking those rules. Although they won't like it at first, consistency in enforcing boundaries provides a sense of security and predictability for your toddler.

3. *Define your own boundaries.* Besides setting boundaries for your child, it's equally important to have a set of personal boundaries based on your values and beliefs. Children learn by observing their parents, so modeling the behaviors and values you want to instill in them is essential. For instance, if honesty is a core value, demonstrate it in your actions rather than just talking about it. Children are more likely to follow the rules if they see you living by the same principles.

4. *Discuss reasons for the boundaries.* Engage your child in discussions about your family's guiding principles. Encourage them to voice their opinions and be part of the decision-making process, if appropriate. When they understand the reasons, they are more likely to follow the rules.

5. *Allow room for negotiation.* While consistency is essential, it's also crucial to allow room for negotiation within reasonable boundaries. By letting your toddler choose or even create the rules and boundaries, they will be more likely to respect them. It's also useful, depending on your child, to let them set a boundary or two for you as a dad. That way, if they don't adhere to the boundary, you can tell them you won't follow their rules, either.

6. *Recognize good behaviors.* Focus on positive reinforcement by acknowledging and praising your child when they follow the rules and show positive behavior. Recognizing their efforts and achievements helps build their self-esteem and reinforces the importance of adhering to boundaries.

7. *Let them experience consequences.* When your child crosses a boundary, it's important to let them experience the natural consequences of their actions. For instance, if they cannot complete their chores before a promised reward, follow through with not providing the reward. This teaches them the importance of accountability and helps them understand that actions have consequences.

8. *Don't focus on mistakes.* When your child makes a poor choice and crosses a boundary, remind them of the consequences without dwelling on their

mistake. Express empathy for their feelings but also encourage them to make better choices in the future. Avoid excessive scolding or criticism, as this can be counterproductive.[5]

DAD DISCIPLINE

If you're hesitant about disciplining your toddler because you don't want to be seen as the *Big Bad Dad*, let me assure you that the opposite is more likely to be true. You are actually strengthening your long-term relationship with your child or children. (But, yes, they will resent the rules at first, and you will sometimes be in unpleasant conflict with them.)

These challenges will be easier (but not easy) if you discipline yourself first—i.e., show your child **the** desired behavior instead of just telling them what not to do.[6] For example, if you want them to use gentle hands, demonstrate gentle touching and explain why it's important. You should also encourage your toddler to express their feelings and thoughts—they must never feel that a boundary means they can't talk to you. As much as possible, give them your full and undivided attention when they're telling you something. This makes them less likely to engage in negative behavior. Concomitantly, when they display good behavior, praise them for it. Positive reinforcement can be more effective than focusing solely on poor behavior.

Bear in mind that misbehavior can be a way for your toddler to communicate frustration or discomfort. Listen to their concerns and acknowledge their feelings, even if you ultimately need to enforce a consequence. Consequences should be age- and temperament-appropriate and related to the misbehavior.

Here are some other methods for maintaining discipline:

1. *Call a time-out.* When your child crosses a boundary, calmly explain why their behavior was not acceptable and then place them in a designated time-out area for a brief period (usually one minute per year of age). This gives them a chance to reflect on their actions and provides a space to regain control of their emotions. Use this time to allow them to calm down and reflect on their actions. Offer them a chance to make amends afterward.

2. *Redirect.* Instead of simply saying "No," offer an alternative behavior or activity. For example, if your child is playing too roughly, redirect them to a more appropriate activity or toy. This approach helps them learn what is acceptable and positively redirects their energy. Timing plays a critical role; identifying signs of restlessness, irritability, or potential conflicts between siblings can help defuse situations before they escalate.

3. *Allocate one-on-one time.* Devoting individualized time to your child is crucial for fostering strong relationships. This can be as short as 20 minutes a day or even just five minutes. You can incorporate it into daily tasks like washing dishes together or casual conversations during chores. The key is to eliminate distractions, such as turning off the TV and phone and fully engaging with your child at their level.

4. *Establish clear expectations.* Instead of instructing your child on what not to do, specify what you want them to do. Clear and concise directions, such as "Please gather all your toys and place them in the toy box," establish precise expectations, increasing the likelihood of compliance. However, it's essential to set realistic goals, recognizing your child's capabilities. Requesting the impossible sets them up for failure.[7]

Part of a child's development involves understanding the consequences of their actions. Explain the potential outcomes of their misbehavior and provide a warning, allowing them an opportunity to rectify their conduct. When he was three, Tyler started scribbling on the walls of our apartment. I could stop him by telling him he wouldn't be allowed to play with his favorite toy (a transformer truck back then) if he continued drawing on the wall.

As with tantrums, it's important to never get angry. Consistency is also important, as it creates a positive feedback loop and helps children grasp the cause-and-effect relationship between their behavior and consequences.

MAKING A DIY TODDLER

The aim of establishing boundaries is to foster a child who does what you want without having to be told. You want them to make the right choices and decisions independently. This is a fundamental aspect of a child's development. Encouraging autonomy in toddlers not only empowers them but also lays the foundation for their future as confident, responsible, and self-reliant individuals.

As I already noted, one way to foster this attitude is by giving your toddler a say in family decisions and activities. This builds respect, strengthens the parent-child bond, invites cooperation, nurtures problem-solving skills, and, maybe most important of all, recognizes children's innate need for power and control.

You can establish a regular family ritual or meeting where everyone voices their opinions and preferences. This can be a weekly meal planning session or a discussion about weekend activities. Having a dedicated time for family input reinforces the importance of their voices. When children are included in discussions and decisions, they feel respected and valued. This builds a foundation of mutual respect within the family and teaches children how to treat others respectfully.

While the family unit is, ultimately, not a democracy, it can be the place where recognition of everyone's rights is established. Giving kids a say helps them develop problem-solving and critical-thinking skills. They learn to consider options, weigh pros and cons, and make informed choices.[8]There's also the practical aspect that including children in decision-making can lead to a greater willingness to participate in tasks and activities. This is no trivial thing when you want them to dry the dishes, mop, and chop your calves after a long run.

These are some benefits of the autonomy approach to parenting:

- *Developed Sense of Self:* Autonomy allows children to explore their preferences, interests, and identities. When they make choices, they begin to form a sense of self, helping them understand who they are and what they like.
- *Improved Confidence:* Making decisions and experiencing the consequences, whether positive or negative, boosts a toddler's confidence. Autonomy allows them to see the impact of their choices, fostering a sense of control and competence.
- *Command Over Their Minds and Bodies:* Autonomy enables children to understand their capabilities

and limitations. They learn to regulate their thoughts, emotions, and behaviors, leading to better self-control and emotional intelligence.

- *Critical Thinking:* Encouraging autonomy involves problem-solving and decision-making, which are crucial aspects of critical thinking. As toddlers learn to weigh options and consequences, their cognitive skills are sharpened.
- *Self-motivation:* Autonomy nurtures intrinsic motivation. When children choose activities or tasks based on their interests, they are more likely to be self-driven, eager to learn, and enthusiastic about their pursuits.
- *Increased Responsibility:* As children exercise autonomy, they also learn to take responsibility for their choices. This helps them understand the importance of accountability and consequences.

To foster autonomy, provide opportunities for your toddler to make choices within boundaries. For example, let them choose their outfit for the day, a snack from a selection, or a book to read. However, while I highly recommend this approach, it needs to be carefully calibrated. Don't overwhelm your child with choices. Too many choices can lead to confusion and frustration. Offer age-appropriate options and limit the number of decisions they need to make.

Design your child's environment to support independence. For instance, you can arrange toys and materials that encourage exploration and self-directed play. Provide safe spaces where they can move freely and explore their surroundings. It's also important that, when your child faces difficulties or conflicts, you refrain from immediately intervening. Too many parents fail to realize that children are often not helped by our help. So, give them space to solve problems on their own. Offer guidance and support if needed, but allow them to experience overcoming obstacles.

Remember to express gratitude for your child's contributions and choices. When children feel appreciated for their input, they are more likely to remain engaged and enthusiastic about participating in family decisions. Positive reinforcement encourages continued involvement. Incorporating these guidelines into your parenting approach can create a harmonious family environment where children feel empowered, respected, and valued. It fosters cooperation, encourages problem-solving, and allows children to satisfy their natural need for control healthily and constructively.

Moreover, it strengthens the bonds within the family, emphasizing the importance of every member's voice and input in shaping family life. Ultimately, giving kids a say not only benefits them individually but also enriches the family, creating a supportive and inclusive atmosphere where everyone's needs and preferences are considered and respected.

Autonomy is not only a gift we give to our children but also a skill that will serve them well throughout their lives.

KEY TAKEAWAYS

- Boundaries help set your toddler's foundation for adult life by teaching about rules.
- Use boundaries to teach your toddler to be self-reliant by letting them help set the rules.
- Enforce the boundaries when your child flouts them.

Boundaries facilitate family harmony and, by so doing, strengthen the family bonds between parents and children. In the next chapter, we explore more ways to deepen your connection with your child.

PART III

THE DYNAMICS OF FAMILY LIFE

7

A DAD'S GUIDE TO A CLOSE-KNIT FAMILY

Michael J. Fox, who was diagnosed with Parkinson's disease when he was just 29 years old, once said, "Family is not an important thing. It's everything." I think this is something we only realize after we have our own children. Even if we have a good relationship with our parents and siblings, we don't fully appreciate what our own parents did for us until we become parents ourselves. For me, and I am sure for many of the dads reading this book, the man we were before and the father we are now are almost completely different individuals.

This is why family is "everything." Fox has four children, all born after his diagnosis.[1] Unless we're involved in some grand project, like curing cancer, writing the Great American Substack, or winning the World Tiddlywinks championship, it is our children who make our lives meaningful and give us purpose. And what is life without purpose and meaning? Ask the depressed, the drug addict, the Atlanta Falcons. This is why it's important to have good relationships with our birth family and to build good relationships with our children.

Family is mostly the foundation of our life, both emotionally and practically. Family are the people who are always there for you, from your parents to your brothers and sisters. And, if we didn't have that kind of family, that's more reason to make sure our kids do.

In life, we're going to face challenges and bad times. When that happens, family is the best anchor to keep us steady and to keep us striving. So, how do we ensure we build a good relationship with our child or children as they grow?

TIME AFTER TIME

When our children grow up and move out on their own, they will carry with them memories of time spent with their parents, both good and bad. That's why it's so important for dads to make sure they don't spend so many hours working that they diminish or even lose their relationship with their kids.

Let's look at some of the real benefits of spending time with family.*Strengthens family bonding*: One benefit of indulging in leisure activities with your children is that it strengthens the family bond. This is so for all types of family activities, such as game night, movie night, gardening, or playing outdoors.

- *Molds the children's future parenting skills*: Kids learn by example (but not necessarily yours). Still, if you set a good example of how to behave with your children, your son or daughter will remember that. Hopefully, they will naturally apply these 'parenting skills' in the future with their children. In fact, you will probably notice siblings treating each other in the ways you treat them. Ashley often tells Tyler, "Would you like it if someone did that to you? Don't do something you wouldn't like done to you." We never explicitly taught her the Golden Rule.

- *Increased happiness*: Developing a sense of belonging as a child is an enormous benefit of family that stays with you throughout your life. That sense of belonging can make children happier. A benefit of family time is learning that we are cared for and needed, and both elements are important to happiness. Families need all their members to be an active part of the circle to function at their best.

- *More confident children*: Another benefit of family time can be building self-confidence. When parents display self-confidence that shows they have a positive value of themselves without putting others down, kids can learn to value themselves. Family can foster a healthy self-esteem and a positive self-concept. This occurs not only through modeling behavior but also through helping the child develop important skills. Social competence and problem-solving skills naturally improve the child's self-confidence.[2]

PLAY IT FORWARD

In the early years, your child's primary way of learning and developing is through play. So, by playing with them, you not only help them learn but also form a dad-play-mate relationship with them. In fact, dads typically play with their children more than mothers, and that's often the basis for the father-son *and* father-daughter bond.[3]

Nurturing and affectionate exchanges between you and your child fosters your child's self-assurance, resilience, and communication skills. These skills are essential for your child in adulthood for problem-solving, stress management, and establishing healthy relationships.[4]

Play is a crucial aspect of development and relationship building in the early years. It's not just enjoyable for your child but also provides an opportunity for exploration, observation, experimentation, problem-solving, and learning from mistakes.

Your relationship enhances the benefits of play for your child. Your encouragement boosts your child's confidence to explore, experiment, and learn from mistakes. Spending ample time playing, talking, listening, and interacting with you also helps your child acquire essential life skills like communication, thinking, problem-solving, movement, and socializing with other children and adults.[5]

Playing with your toddler not only strengthens the bond between father and child but also plays a crucial role in their development. Here are four simple strategies that you can use as a dad can use to interact effectively with your child:

1. *Pause and listen.* When conversing with your toddler, it's important to pause after you speak to give your child an opportunity to respond. This not only encourages your child to express their thoughts and feelings but also teaches them the rhythm of conversation. It shows them that their words are valued and that communication is a two-way process.
2. *Comment on play.* Playtime is an excellent opportunity for interaction. While playing with your toddler, comment on what your child is doing without trying to change their actions. For example, if your child is building a tower with blocks, you might say, 'Wow, that's a tall tower!

How many more blocks before it falls down?' This type of commentary encourages your child to think critically about their actions and fosters their problem-solving skills. It also shows your child that you are interested in their activities and thoughts.

3. *Provide positive reinforcement.* This is a powerful tool in shaping behavior. When your child does something you like, tell them specifically what you appreciate about their action. For example, if your child helps pick up the blocks after playtime, you might say, 'I love it when you help pick up the blocks.' This not only encourages good behavior but also boosts your child's self-esteem. It shows them that their actions have an impact and that they can make positive contributions.

4. *Be present.* Perhaps the most important aspect of interacting with your toddler is simply being present. Engage with your child in their world. Get down on their level, make eye contact, and show genuine interest in what they're doing. This sends a powerful message to your child: *You are important, and I value our time together.*

MAKING MEMORIES

Engaging in shared activities as a family, regardless of their nature or cost, can significantly enhance familial ties. This applies to all forms of family engagements, which don't have to be extravagant or expensive. Shared experiences foster emotional closeness among family members and form lasting memories for your child.

Here are some activities that families can do together:

- *Cooking:* this not only teaches children valuable life skills but also provides an opportunity for families to bond over a shared task.
- *Reading:* whether it's a bedtime story for younger children or a book club for older ones, reading together can foster a love of literature and stimulate intellectual conversations.
- *Chores:* while it might not sound like fun, doing chores together can teach responsibility and teamwork. It also provides an opportunity for families to work towards a common goal.
- *Exercising:* whether it's a walk in the park, a bike ride, or a yoga session at home, exercising together promotes health and well-being while also providing quality family time.
- *Craft and DIY projects:* these activities can foster creativity and result in tangible memories of time spent together.

Remember, the goal of these activities is to spend quality time together, strengthen bonds, and create lasting memories.

Spending time with family is not just about fun and bonding; it also plays a crucial role in helping children develop parenting skills. When children engage in activities with their parents and siblings, they are exposed to a variety of situations that allow them to observe and learn important life skills.

When children see their parents nurturing their siblings, resolving conflicts, or managing household chores, they are indirectly learning how to handle similar situations. They learn about responsibility when they see their parents juggling work and home life. They understand the importance of empathy and compassion when they see their parents caring for a sick sibling or comforting a distressed family member.

Taking part in family activities also provides children with opportunities to practice these skills. For instance, older siblings often help care for younger ones, which can include tasks like feeding, bathing, or helping with homework. This not only teaches them practical skills but also helps them understand the responsibilities that come with caring for another person.

Spending time as a family allows for open communication. Parents can use this time to discuss various topics, including those related to parenting. They can discuss why certain rules are in place or why specific behaviors are encouraged or discouraged. Such discussions can provide children with a deeper understanding of the thought processes and considerations involved in parenting decisions.

As children get older, they understand more of what you say, as well as how you say it. Here are some tips for positive attention for your toddler:

- Get into the moment with your toddler. This could be as simple as crouching down to look at a caterpillar together.
- When you're talking with your toddler, leave time after you talk so your child can reply.
- Tell your child exactly what you like about what they're doing. For example, "I love it when you help to pick up the blocks."

If you have more than one child, though, chances are they're not going to be so agreeable with each other.

SIBLING RIVALRY: A STORY OF THE NEW WEST

On a typical Saturday morning, seven-year-old Ashley got into a heated argument with her five-year-old brother Tyler over who would get the coveted spot on Daddy's lap to watch SpongeBob SquarePants.

"Daddy, I want to sit on your lap!" she shouted.

Tyler immediately asserted himself. "But I want to sit there!"

"Alright, kids," I said. "How about this? Each of you will get a turn, but whoever can tell me a SpongeBob joke can sit first for five minutes.

Ashley was quick off the mark. "Why did SpongeBob go to the party?" she asked.

"I don't know. Why did SpongeBob go to the party?"

"Because he's a fungi!" she giggled. ("Fun guy.")

I don't think Tyler got it, but he smiled anyway and sat quietly by my side until it was his turn.

Some experts say sibling rivalry stems from children competing for their parents' love. Others say the children" goal is parental recognition or attention. However, sibling rivalry does not occur in all cultures.[6] In many societies, older children take care of the younger ones, and sibling rivalry doesn't occur. Only when families started having just two or three children, and toys for each one became standard practice, did sibling rivalry become a phenomenon.

If you have more than one child, it's something you, as a parent, have to deal with. One solution is to have your second child soon after your first. While Ashley and Tyler do have their conflicts, they are also as close as any two human beings can be, and I see them having a relationship later in life where they know there's always one other person in the world who has their back.

Here are the six common reasons for sibling rivalry:

Attention and approval: Siblings often compete for their parents' attention and approval. They may feel that their sibling is favored or receives more attention, leading to feelings of jealousy and rivalry.

1. *Individual temperaments*: The individual temperaments of each sibling can play a significant role in sibling rivalry. For example, one child may be easygoing while the other is more assertive, leading to conflicts.

2. *Age and developmental differences*: Age and developmental differences can also contribute to sibling rivalry. Older siblings may feel burdened with responsibilities, while younger siblings may feel overshadowed or left out.

3. *Shared resources*: Competition over shared resources, such as toys or time spent with parents, can lead to rivalry.

4. *Parental behavior*: Parents' behavior can inadvertently contribute to sibling rivalry. For instance, comparing siblings or labeling them (like "the smart one" or "the athletic one") can foster competition.

5. *Life changes*: Major life changes like a new baby, divorce, or a move can increase stress and trigger sibling rivalry.

While sibling rivalry is normal to some extent, it's important for parents to manage it effectively to ensure it doesn't escalate into persistent conflict. These are the red flags you need to look out for:

- Calling each other names
- Telling on each other
- Verbal sparring, but not good-naturedly
- Poking or hitting each other
- Breaking or hiding each other's possessions

It is normal for siblings to have disagreements and conflicts. However, it's important for parents to manage these situations effectively. Here are some strategies parents can use to deal with sibling rivalry:

- *Avoid comparisons.* Each child is unique, with their own strengths and weaknesses. Avoid comparing your children to each other, as this can foster feelings of inadequacy and resentment. Instead, celebrate each child's individual achievements and progress.
- *Understand the causes of conflicts.* Try to figure out what's behind sibling conflicts. Is it a fight over a toy, jealousy over attention, or something else? Understanding the root cause can help you address the issue effectively.
- *Appreciate differences.* Teach your children to appreciate each other's differences. Encourage

them to respect and value their sibling's unique qualities and perspectives.

- *Team up for chores.* Having siblings work together on chores can foster teamwork and cooperation. It provides an opportunity for them to work towards a common goal and can help reduce rivalry.
- *Improve listening skills.* Good communication is key to resolving conflicts. Teach your children active listening skills. This involves not just hearing the words but also understanding the emotions behind them.
- *Teach respect.* Respect is fundamental in any relationship. Teach your children the importance of treating each other with kindness and consideration.
- *Disagree respectfully.* It's okay to have different opinions. Show your children how to express their disagreements in a respectful and constructive manner.
- *Emphasize family bonding.* Regular family activities can strengthen bonds and reduce conflicts. Whether it's a family meal, a game night, or a weekend outing, these shared experiences can bring siblings closer together.
- *Make time for fun.* Ensure there's plenty of time for fun and relaxation. A positive and joyful environment can reduce tension and promote better relationships among siblings.

- *Conflict resolution.* Discuss ways of handling conflicts with your children. Teach them conflict resolution skills such as taking turns, compromising, and apologizing when they're wrong. Role-play different scenarios with them to practice these skills.

On conflict resolution, I found two strategies especially effective: the red light and the solution jar. Introduce the concept of a traffic light to your child. Request your child to visualize a traffic light with their eyes closed. When the red light is illuminated, they should take three deep breaths and think of a soothing image. As the light changes to yellow, it's time to assess the situation. They should consider if they can manage the situation independently or if they require help from an adult. They should also brainstorm two potential solutions to the problem. When the light turns green, they should select a strategy (such as seeking help, going outside for a run, or working towards a compromise) and implement it.

The red light serves as a calming mechanism, enabling children to better comprehend the problem and select an appropriate strategy. Practicing this traffic light technique during calm moments can aid in reinforcing this process in your child's memory.

When your child approaches you to discuss a problem with a friend, ensure you are at eye level with your child and show empathy. Acknowledge their feelings by saying something like, "It seems like you had a tough day with your friend. I can sense that you're upset and frustrated." This shows your child that you are listening to and understanding their feelings. It's normal for children to experience intense emotions; what's important is how they navigate through these emotions. Seeking support from a parent is an excellent coping mechanism.

Listening and empathizing are beneficial strategies at the moment. Parents don't need to fix every problem. In fact, it's better if they don't. Providing a safe space for children to express and process their emotions is the best support.

Encourage your child to express their feelings in a healthy and calm manner. Young children often react quickly to upsetting events. Quick frustration or blaming are common reactions to friendship troubles with young children.

Encourage your child to use "I feel" statements when they're upset with a friend. When children learn to use these statements, they focus on how a behavior affected them without resorting to blaming.

Then there's the stick solutions. Have your child come up with many potential solutions when brainstorming problem-solving strategies with you. Write them down on popsicle sticks and store them in a jar. The next time your child struggles to come up with a solution to a problem with a peer or sibling, ask them to look through the jar and try one.

KEY TAKEAWAYS

- Your relationship with your children gives your life meaning and purpose.
- Spending time with your children creates memories they will carry into adulthood.
- Sibling rivalry is not inevitable but can be managed if it occurs.

Part of ensuring your children's well-being is making sure you and your partner have a good relationship. Too often, parents let children take over their lives, to everyone's detriment. In the next chapter, we'll look at how you can nurture your romantic relationship while parenting.

8

PARENTING WITHOUT LOSING EACH OTHER

W hen women have a baby, many of them cut back their work hours or, if their financial situation allows, quit entirely. Men often feel an increased sense of urgency to provide for their growing family.

This makes psychological sense. My wife found more fulfillment in childcare, whileI found more fulfillment in providing for our family. One problem that arises when a baby comes is that both partners forget about fulfilling each other.

Jenny and I went through that phase when Ashley was born, but that was mostly a result of dealing with new challenges and sleep deprivation. Luckily, Ashley began sleeping through the night within a month, and aware that we were snapping at each other too often, we took deliberate steps to rekindle our relationship. (Yes, I mean sex.)

Thus, having a baby strengthened our relationship after the initial hiccups, and when Tyler was born, we were prepared to handle all challenges. What I didn't realize was that having a boy was a time bomb for my marriage.

I love both my children equally, but when my son was born, I was slightly more excited. The daughter-father bond, I think most men will admit, differs from the father-son one. I looked forward to showing Tyler how to catch a baseball, tie a lure to a fishhook, and rebuild an engine. Mind you, I didn't know how to do any of these things myself, but I intended to learn just so I could teach him. So, when Tyler reached his toddler years, I started engaging him even more because he could now engage me with me.

Unfortunately, between work and play, this led to me ignoring Jenny (unless I wanted sex). So, we started having the same troubles we had when Ashley was a bawling baby. At first, I didn't recognize what was happening—okay, I didn't recognize it at all—but Jenny finally sat me down one day and told me what's what.

Luckily, we—by which I mean Jenny—already knew what we had to do from our first rodeo. This chapter goes through the process and provides useful tips for repairing and solidifying your relationship. Sometimes, this involves flowers, sometimes handcuffs. It almost always involves apologizing, maybe with some well-timed groveling.

You don't need to do everything here, but use what fits your personality and your relationship. Once you are both committed to maintaining your relationship within the context of having a child, you will work out what works. Let's start by looking at what makes up a healthy romantic relationship.

THE FOUR FOUNDATIONS OF A HEALTHY RELATIONSHIP

There are four keys to keeping your romantic relationship alive after your children arrive to interrupt you.Maintaining a meaningful emotional connection

1. Embracing respectful disagreement
2. Nurturing outside relationships and interests
3. Practicing open and honest communication[1]

Let's delve more deeply into each of these principles.

At the heart of every healthy relationship is a meaningful emotional connection with each other. This might seem obvious, but it's very easy to let the routine of family life substitute for an emotional interaction. This is especially true for men, because we typically express our feelings by doing. Women, however, want us to express our feelings by expressing our feelings. This is unreasonable, but we have to comply. In a healthy relationship, both partners actively invest time and effort to connect on an emotional level. They listen, empathize, and provide emotional support when needed. This emotional connection acts as the foundation for trust, intimacy, and love.

This doesn't happen without arguing, though. Contrary to popular belief, disagreement can be a healthy and constructive aspect of any relationship. In fact, according to psychologist John Gottman, a leading expert on relationships, a ratio of five positive interactions to one negative one predicts a lasting marriage.[2] More interestingly, a ratio of 11:1 positive interactions also predicted marital breakdown—in other words, we need some conflict to have a good relationship.[3]

Here are some ways to keep the *right ratio*:

- *Be interested.* When your partner expresses dissatisfaction, do you truly listen? Are you genuinely curious about the reasons behind their frustration? Demonstrating interest involves asking open-ended questions and conveying your attentiveness through subtle cues like nods, eye contact, and timely affirmations that signal your deep engagement.
- *Be affectionate.* Do you hold hands, exchange affectionate kisses, or warmly embrace your partner during daily interactions? If you're having an argument, physical and verbal displays of affection can ease stress. Imagine your partner, during a challenging conversation, taking your

hand and saying, "This is difficult, but I love you, and I know we can fix this." This can ease tension and draw you closer. She might pull away her hand and snap that she's not a broken faucet, but hey, take a chance.

- *Be needy.* Okay, not too needy, but you must show your partner that you need them in your life. They often find the key to sustaining a marriage, as somebody put it, in small things done frequently. A look, a touch, a cup of chai tea. Even when you disagree, raising issues that matter to your partner signals your commitment to their well-being and shows your concern. How you treat each other outside of conflicts plays a pivotal role in handling inevitable disagreements more effectively. For example, picking up dinner for your partner on a tough day shows them you're thinking of them. These small gestures accumulate over time, providing a reservoir of positivity in your marriage that can counterbalance the negatives during conflicts.

- *Be appreciative.* Your thoughts about your partner can shape how you treat them. By concentrating on the positive aspects of your marriage, such as cherished memories and your partner's admirable qualities, you infuse your relationship with positive energy. Negativity may creep in, especially during conflicts, but deliberately focusing on the positive can counteract those moments when finding something good about your partner becomes challenging. Translating your thoughts into actions, such as giving your partner compliments, no matter how small, strengthens your relationship.

- *Be one with your partner.* During arguments, it's easy to focus on the negative aspects and overlook points of agreement. Instead, make it a point to find common ground. This shows your spouse that you recognize their viewpoint as valid and also reflects your care for them. Even minor alignment during a conflict can significantly alter how couples engage in disagreements. This doesn't mean that you necessarily consider your partner's viewpoint, but acknowledging that it makes sense to them shows respect. Summarizing your spouse's experience during a conflict, even when you disagree, signals your acknowledgment without implying agreement.

- *Be apologetic.* Empathy serves as a profound avenue for human connection. When you empathize with your spouse, you convey understanding and a shared emotional experience, whether through verbal expressions or nonverbal gestures. Phrases like "I can see why you feel this way" show your solidarity with your partner. Empathy is a skill all romantic partners can and should enhance, with no limit to the amount you can express. If you've upset your partner, a simple apology during the conflict, such as, "I'm sorry for hurting your feelings; I feel bad about that," offers a positive and empathetic interaction that reinforces your bond.

- *Be funny.* Playful teasing, light-heartedness, and shared moments of laughter can diffuse tension during heated disagreements. Know where to draw the line, though, so if your partner doesn't like your jokes, don't try this at home.[4]

Keep in mind that a good relationship doesn't mean an absence of conflict but that the conflict is conducted with rules and, above all, a commitment to your relationship. Both partners should feel free to express their opinions and perspectives, even if they differ on fundamental issues like whether pineapple belongs on pizza. (No, obviously.) Respectful disagreement means valuing each other's viewpoints and working towards a compromise or solution that respects both your needs and boundaries (half pineapple; the other half can be tasty). This approach not only strengthens the relationship but also allows for personal growth and learning.

Then there's not letting family become your sole focus, which is what I had done with Tyler. This strategy was especially healthy for me. I felt the need to get out of the home more than my wife did. But you should also encourage your spouse to pursue some non-family activity. This not only enriches their lives individually but also brings fresh perspectives and experiences to the relationship, especially if you encourage them to do pole-dancing classes. When each partner keeps their unique identity, they have more to share and contribute to the partnership.

The third horseman is one men typically find most difficult. Open and honest communication is the lifeblood of any healthy relationship. It is the channel through which emotions, needs, and concerns are shared. Effective communication involves not only speaking but also active listening. My father was especially good at pretending to listen, and my mother was good at pretending she didn't know he was pretending. Which I think accounts for my parents' happy marriage. Unfortunately, this technique isn't so effective with modern women. Partners should feel safe and comfortable discussing their thoughts and feelings without fear of judgment or reprisal, even if they think *Game of Thrones* is better than *The Walking Dead*. In a healthy relationship, there is a commitment to transparency, authenticity, and realistic zombies.

Always remember healthy relationships are not the result of chance or luck—you have to build your relationship through deliberate actions and choices. Maintain a meaningful emotional connection, embrace respectful disagreement, and practice open and honest communication. These elements form the solid foundation upon which love, trust, and companionship can flourish.

ROMANCING THE DISHES

A good relationship relies on logistics as much as romance. Maybe more. After all, you must do routine household tasks every day. Making love, on the other hand, not so much, unless you're really lucky and have shares in Pfizer. Therefore, working out who does what for both housework and childcare helps keep your relationship on a steady footing. The following is just a general guide that you can adapt to your household.

Work together.

The foundation of any successful division of domestic duties and childcare is teamwork. Couples should approach this challenge as a joint effort, acknowledging that both partners play crucial roles in maintaining a balanced and harmonious household. This shared commitment to working together forms the basis for effective cooperation and problem-solving.

Rethink your goals.

Before diving into the details of who does what, take some time to rethink your goals as a couple. Discuss your long-term vision for your family and how you want to raise your child. Clarify your individual priorities and expectations, and ensure that you are on the same page regarding your family's values and objectives. This shared vision will guide your decisions and division of responsibilities.

List your responsibilities.

Create a comprehensive list of all household chores and childcare tasks, from cooking and cleaning to diaper changes and bedtime routines. Include everything, no matter how small or routine it may seem. This list will serve as a reference point for identifying who is responsible for each task and assessing whether the division of duties is equitable.

List your child's needs.

In addition to your responsibilities, make a list of your child's needs and routines. Children thrive on consistency, so understanding their schedules and requirements is essential. This list will help both partners stay informed and involved in the care of the baby, ensuring that nothing is overlooked.

Anticipate and communicate.

Open and honest communication is key to maintaining a harmonious relationship while sharing domestic duties and childcare. Anticipate potential sources of conflict and address them proactively. Discuss your expectations, concerns, and preferences with your partner. Regularly check in with each other to ensure that both partners feel heard and supported.

Make a schedule.

Create a flexible but structured schedule that outlines when each partner is responsible for specific tasks. This schedule should encompass daily, weekly, and monthly duties, taking into account work commitments and personal preferences. Having a clear schedule provides a sense of predictability and helps avoid misunderstandings or resentment.

Shed traditional expectations.

Traditional gender roles and expectations can be limiting and counterproductive. Embrace a more egalitarian approach to domestic duties and childcare. Recognize that both partners are equally capable of performing any task, whether it's cooking, cleaning, or changing diapers. Challenge outdated stereotypes and ensure that responsibilities are assigned based on individual strengths and availability rather than gender norms.

Share toddler time.

Caring for a baby is a bonding experience that both partners should share. Allocate dedicated "baby time" for each of you to spend quality moments with your child. This not only strengthens the parent-child relationship but also allows both partners to share the joys and challenges of parenting.

Make room for two experts.

Acknowledge that both you and your partner have unique skills, preferences, and approaches to domestic duties and childcare. Instead of competing, celebrate these differences. Be open to learning from each other and recognize that having two experts can lead to a more balanced and harmonious household.

Consider hiring help.

There may be times when the demands of work, childcare, and household responsibilities become overwhelming. In such cases, consider hiring outside help, such as a babysitter, house cleaner, or meal delivery service. Outsourcing certain tasks can reduce stress and free up valuable time for you and your partner to focus on each other and your child.

Let go of perfection.

Parenting and household management are challenging, and it's essential to let go of the expectation of perfection. Accept that there will be messy moments, unexpected challenges, and days when you feel overwhelmed.

Reward yourself.

Finally, don't forget to reward yourselves for your hard work and dedication. Celebrate your achievements, both big and small. Treat yourselves to a date night, indulge in your favorite activities, or simply take a moment to appreciate each other's contributions. These rewards can serve as positive reinforcement for maintaining a harmonious relationship while dividing domestic duties and childcare.[5]

5 TIPS TO KEEP YOUR RELATIONSHIP THRIVING

"What attracts us to a woman rarely binds us to her," wrote the British literary critic John Churton Collins, who lived in the nineteenth century and could thus write such things. No doubt, the same is true of women, especially if the man loses his job.[6] That apart, though, here are five tips on how to stay in love after falling in love.

Tip 1: Spend quality time together.

In the early stages of a relationship, couples often spend countless hours together, exploring each other's worlds and enjoying shared experiences. However, as time passes, life's demands can lead to busy schedules and reduced quality time together. To stay in love, it's essential to prioritize spending quality time face-to-face. Carve out moments to connect and rekindle the emotional bond that brought you together. Whether it's a romantic dinner, a weekend getaway, or simply unwinding together after a long day, these moments of togetherness can reignite the spark and strengthen your connection.

Tip 2: Stay connected through communication.

Effective communication is the lifeblood of any successful relationship. It's not enough to rely solely on physical presence; maintaining an emotional connection is equally vital. Regular and open communication allows you to share your thoughts, feelings, and concerns. Attempt to check in with each other, ask about your partner's day, and actively listen to what they have to say. Communication builds understanding and empathy, fostering a deeper connection. It's essential to address any issues or conflicts promptly rather than allowing them to fester and potentially harm your relationship.

Tip 3: Keep physical intimacy alive.

Physical intimacy plays a crucial role in romantic relationships. While the intensity of physical attraction may ebb and flow over time, it's important to keep the flame of physical intimacy alive. This includes both sexual and non-sexual forms of physical affection. Regular physical contact, such as hugs, kisses, cuddling, and holding hands, can reinforce your emotional connection. Intimacy is a powerful way to express love and desire, so prioritize it in your relationship to maintain the passion that initially drew you together.

Tip 4: Learn to give and take in your relationship.

Every relationship involves compromise and sacrifice. To stay in love, it's essential to learn the art of give-and-take. Both partners should make concessions and prioritize each other's happiness. This means understanding that your partner's needs and desires are equally important as your own. Be negotiable and find solutions that work for both of you. The ability to give and take fosters a sense of equity and strengthens the bond between you.

Tip 5: Be prepared for ups and downs.

No relationship is without its challenges. Difficulties are a natural part of any long-term partnership. To stay in love, it's crucial to be prepared for these fluctuations and approach them with resilience and patience. During tough times, remember the love and commitment that brought you together initially. Seek support from each other, friends, or a therapist if needed. By weathering the storms together, you can emerge from difficult periods with an even stronger connection and a deeper appreciation for each other.[7]

KEY TAKEAWAYS

- Be careful you don't put your children above your relationship.
- Ups and downs are normal in relationships.
- Healthy relationships are just as much about logistics as romance.
- Make a plan and put time and effort into it.

Love is a journey, not just an emotion. It's a continuous process of growth and connection that endures and thrives over time. By working on your relationship with each other, you are nurturing your family. We look in the final chapter at a commonly overlooked phenomenon: parental burnout.

9

RECHARGING THE DAD BATTERY

Don't sacrifice yourself too much, because if you sacrifice too much there's nothing else you can give, and nobody will care for you."

— *KARL LAGERFELD*

As I mentioned in the previous chapter, men work harder when they become fathers. This carries two risks: one, work may undermine our budding relationship with our child, and two, we may exhaust ourselves trying to provide for our family. This chapter deals with the latter and tells you what you can do to avoid dad burnout.

The recognition of parental burnout is a relatively recent phenomenon, and dad burnout is even newer. In the early 1980s, Belgian psychology researchers Isabelle Roskam and Moïra Mikolajczak coined the term "parental burnout." They described this phenomenon as "an exhaustion syndrome" characterized by three distinct aspects: overwhelming exhaustion related to parenting, emotional distance from one's children, and a sense of ineffectiveness as a parent.[1]

I'm pretty sure our grandparents never suffered from this syndrome. So what changed between their generation and ours? Did our parents turn into snowflakes and then raise a snowfall of young adults who can only parent with the help of therapy?

Not really. The fact is, we as parents now face pressures our grandparents, and even our own parents, never had to deal with. It's important to understand the source of these pressures and, even more importantly, to cope with them —for ourselves and our children.

NEW DAD, OLD DAD

In the evolving landscape of parenting, American mothers and fathers are dedicating more time to their children than ever before.

This might not be a problem if that extra time was devoted to nurturing your relationships with your kids. But a lot of it is parental *work* rather than parental *play* and our toddlers like nothing more than playing with their parents. But, for play to be fun, both playmates must enjoy it, right?

Here's the problem. It's not that we new parents are less effective parents than our grandparents or parents—it's that our ideas about what a good parent is, or should be, have changed. And these new ideas aren't necessarily correct.

As one study put it, "What parents feed their children, how they discipline them, where they put them to bed, how they play with them: all of these have become politically and morally charged questions. The expectations towards parents have drastically evolved over the last 50 years, to such an extent that parents who would have been considered as good and attentive parents 50 years ago would now be viewed as neglectful at best."[2]

Parental burnout is a particularly Western problem. Unlike other societies, parenting is now "child-centered, expert-guided, emotionally absorbing, labor-intensive, and financially expensive."[3] We're now expected to both reduce the slightest risks to offspring and to optimize our children's physical, intellectual, social, and emotional development, which is not only impossible but not even good for our children. As one scholar puts it, "The distinction between what children need and what might enhance their development has disappeared, and anything less than optimal parenting is framed as perilous."[4]

Now, perhaps the world differs from what it was in our grandparents' and even our parents' day. That's true. More to the point, we parents must realize that if we spend some time on ourselves, we're not going to ruin our children's lives. So, let's start with a self-examination to see if we're taking our parenting too seriously and are in danger of burning out.

ARE YOU A ROCKET MAN?

What are the risk factors for parental burnout? The list below might make you immediately conclude that you have parental burnout since these appear to be a pretty standard description of being a man and father. That's not necessarily the case, but you must decide for yourself if these factors are harming your health and happiness. If so, you need to act. Let's review.

1. *Overwhelming responsibilities*: One of the primary causes of parental burnout is the overwhelming burden of responsibilities that modern parents face. Balancing work, household chores, and childcare can be incredibly demanding. Juggling these responsibilities can lead to intense physical and mental exhaustion, leaving you feeling drained and tired all the time.
2. *Lack of support*: Inadequate support systems can also contribute to parental burnout. Many parents feel isolated and alone in their caregiving roles.

When they lack a strong support network of friends, family, or community resources, they may experience emotional detachment and feelings of being trapped. This isolation can exacerbate their stress levels and lead to burnout.

3. *Perfectionism and unrealistic expectations*: Unrealistic expectations and perfectionism can also fuel parental burnout. In today's social media-driven culture, parents are bombarded with images and stories of perfect families and parents who appear to effortlessly handle every aspect of their lives. This can create an unattainable standard that parents feel compelled to meet. When they fall short of these expectations, they may experience feelings of inadequacy and a loss of a sense of accomplishment related to parenting.

4. *Neglecting self-care*: Parents caught up in the whirlwind of daily responsibilities often neglect self-care. When parents do not prioritize self-care, they become more susceptible to burnout. Signs of burnout, such as increased addictive behaviors like drinking or smoking, can emerge as parents seek unhealthy coping mechanisms to escape the overwhelming demands of taking care of their children.

5. *Financial stress*: Financial pressures can also contribute to parental burnout. The cost of raising children, coupled with economic uncertainties, can lead to anxiety and stress. Financial worries

can escalate conflict between parents, adding to the strain on the family unit.

6. *Sleep deprivation and health issues*: The physical toll of parenting is significant, with sleep deprivation being a common issue. Parents facing burnout often experience sleep disorders and other health problems, such as headaches and muscle aches. These physical symptoms can further exacerbate their emotional and mental exhaustion.

7. *Relationship strain*: Parental burnout can strain relationships between parents themselves. The increased irritability and frustration that parents may exhibit can lead to more frequent and intense conflicts between them. This strained relationship dynamic can worsen feelings of isolation and emotional detachment.

8. *Loss of personal identity*: Another significant cause of parental burnout is the loss of personal identity. As parents dedicate their time and energy to their children, they may lose motivation and interest in activities they used to enjoy. This loss of personal fulfillment and identity can contribute to the overall sense of burnout.[5]

That's a dire list, but the effects could be even worse.

BURNED OUT DAD, BAD TODDLER

Here's the paradox you need to focus on: you get Daddy burnout because you're so focused on your kids, but Daddy burnout means you can't focus on your kids, at least not in the ways they want and need.

Burnout affects both your physical and mental health. Now, the two things that your toddler wants are (a) to play with you and (b) to chat with you. When you're physically exhausted, you can go through the motions of play, and children, being play experts, will know that you're not really into it. (I mean, we never really are into their games, but we're always into them when we're playing.)

It's even worse with chatting. Our kids talk to us to get information, to learn how to converse, and to just interact with Daddy because they love us. If you're mentally not there, they, at best, get only the first, not much of the second, and a disengaged parent for the third. The emotional exhaustion that accompanies burnout can lead to detachment and decreased responsiveness. Your exhaustion and feeling of being overwhelmed can leave you feeling like you're just going through the motions rather than actively participating in your kids' lives. What should be your greatest joy in life becomes your greatest chore. And, if that happens, what's the point of being a parent, right?

If you're not concerned about yourself, be concerned for your kids. Children are perceptive, and they can sense when their parent is emotionally distant. This can sow the seeds of insecurity and confusion in their young minds. The strained parent-child relationship, fueled by burnout, can lead to misunderstandings and strained communication. Kids may feel as though they are not receiving the attention and affection they need. This can lead to a vicious cycle, where your kids' behavior now leads you to feel even more stressed when interacting with them.

None of this will ruin their own relationships with other people, but it may well undermine your father-child bond.

Between trying to balance the demands of work, parenting, and personal life, you may end up creating a cycle of chronic stress. The constant juggling act often leads to feelings of overwhelm, anxiety, and even depression. Sleep deprivation, an inevitable consequence of parenting, can exacerbate these mental health issues.

If you don't take steps to break this pattern, you may pay a heavy health price by the time your kids are grown. Stress-related illnesses such as hypertension, cardiovascular problems, and weakened immune systems become more prevalent among individuals grappling with burnout.

I'm pretty sure you're not running yourself ragged, dropping them to all their various activities and reading them stories and carrying them to the zoo just to end up being the guy who took care of them but who they don't really know. Or a father who doesn't live long enough to see his grandchildren. So, in the next section, we look at some steps you can take.

HOW TO STOP BEING A BURNING MAN

As dads, we cannot allow ourselves to reach a burnout breaking point. So, I put together some things that helped me. Here are ten ways to recover from burnout or stop yourself from even starting down that fiery slope:

1. *Seek professional help.* If you find yourself struggling to cope with the stress and emotional toll of being a new dad, consider seeking professional help. A therapist can provide you with the guidance and tools to navigate this new chapter in your life effectively.
2. *Go outside.* Fresh air and nature can work wonders for your mood and mental health. Whenever you can, take a break from your daily routine and go for a walk, run, or simply sit in the sun. It's a simple yet effective way to recharge your spirit.
3. *Exercise.* Physical activity is a powerful stress reducer and mood enhancer. Devote some time each day to exercise, whether it's at the gym, home workouts, or outdoor activities.
4. *Connect with other dads.* There's immense comfort in talking to fellow dads who understand the

unique challenges and joys of fatherhood. Seek out opportunities to connect with other dads, either in person or online. Sharing experiences and advice can be a tremendous source of support.

5. *Make time for yourself.* In the whirlwind of parenthood, it's easy to neglect your personal interests and hobbies. However, making time for activities that bring you happiness and relaxation is essential. Whether it's reading, listening to music, or spending time in nature, find something that rejuvenates your spirit.

6. *Eat healthy.* Your diet directly impacts your mood and energy levels. Opt for nutritious foods that provide the essential nutrients your body and mind need to thrive. A well-balanced diet will contribute to your overall well-being.

7. *Sleep.* Quality sleep is vital for managing stress and maintaining a positive mood. Prioritize getting enough rest whenever possible. Establish a sleep routine that aligns with your child's schedule to ensure you're well-rested.

8. *Practice meditation or yoga.* Both meditation and yoga are excellent practices for reducing stress and promoting relaxation. There are many resources available, including online classes and apps, to help you get started if you're new to these practices.

9. *Take a break.* When you're feeling overwhelmed, remember to take short breaks to relax and rejuvenate. Whether it's a soothing bath, your favorite music, or simply focusing on your breath for a few minutes, these breaks can make a significant difference in managing stress.

10. *Join a support group.* Consider joining a support group, either in your local community or online. These groups provide a platform for parental experiences, seeking advice, and building connections with other parents who are on a similar journey.[6]

SOMETIMES, IT IS ALL ABOUT YOU

Taking these steps will benefit you and your kids in the long run. When Dads take_some_me_time, they get the following outcomes:

1. *Kids become closer*: Me-time allows fathers to recharge emotionally. It provides a space to relax, unwind, and rejuvenate. When fathers take a break from their busy schedules, they are better able to connect with their children on an emotional level. Increased warmth and sensitivity can lead to deeper, more meaningful interactions with their kids.

2. *A clear head*: A cluttered mind can make decision-making and problem-solving difficult. Me-time

provides an opportunity to clear the mental clutter. Whether it's through meditation, a walk in nature, or simply sitting quietly, this mental clarity can help fathers approach challenges with a fresh perspective.

3. *Get more done*: Paradoxically, taking time for oneself can actually boost productivity. When fathers are well-rested and mentally clear, they can accomplish tasks more efficiently. Me-time can help recharge the energy needed to tackle daily responsibilities with renewed vigor.

4. *Increased creativity*: Me-time often involves activities that promote relaxation and introspection, such as reading, art, or hobbies. Engaging in these activities can stimulate creativity, allowing fathers to explore new ideas and problem-solving approaches.

5. *Better plan for a better man*: Me-time is an ideal opportunity for fathers to reflect on their goals and priorities. It provides a quiet space to plan and strategize for the future. This can be immensely valuable for both personal and family aspirations.

6. *Spouse benefits*: Healthy relationships require a balance between togetherness and personal space. When fathers take me-time, they not only rejuvenate themselves but also create an opportunity for their partner to do the same. This

balance fosters a stronger, more harmonious relationship.

7. *Know thyself*: Me-time is a chance for self-discovery. Fathers can use this time to explore their interests, passions, and values. Self-awareness gained during me-time can lead to personal growth and a deeper sense of fulfillment.[7]

While all this sounds good, the challenge is the same one that got you into this state in the first place: not enough time. But you've got to make the time. Here are some tips:

- Treat me-time as a non-negotiable appointment. Block out time in your calendar and communicate with your family about its importance.
- Me-time doesn't have to be a grand, time-consuming endeavor. Even a few minutes of meditation, a short walk, or indulging in a hobby can make a difference.
- Don't hesitate to share parenting responsibilities with your partner or seek help from family members. This can free up time for your me-time.
- Establish clear boundaries with work and personal commitments. Avoid overextending yourself, which can leave little room for me-time.

WRITE IT DOWN

Active 1: I wrote both this book and my previous one on first-time fathers to help myself as much as to help other dads. You might not have the time or the inclination to write an entire book, but keeping a journal can help keep you focused. Here are a few entries from my journal that summarize some strategies in this chapter.

Journal Entry 1: Mindful Breathing. March 1.

Today, I tried something new to combat my parental burnout—mindful breathing. I took a few minutes in the morning to sit quietly and focus on my breath. It was surprisingly calming, and I felt more centered afterward. I'm going to make this a daily practice.

Journal Entry 2: Prioritizing Sleep. March 7.

I've realized that sleep is a lifeline. Last night, I made an effort to get to bed earlier. I managed a solid 7 hours of sleep, and today, I felt noticeably more energized. I need to make this a habit and not let Netflix keep me up!

Journal Entry 3: Seeking Professional Help. March 15.

Took a big step today—I reached out to a therapist specializing in parental burnout. It was nerve-wracking, but talking about my feelings with someone who understands felt liberating. Looking forward to the upcoming sessions.

Journal Entry 4: Setting Boundaries. March 22.

I've decided to be more assertive about my boundaries. Today, I kindly but firmly told my co-workers that I couldn't work late anymore. It was uncomfortable, but it was a necessary step to create more space for myself and my family.

Journal Entry 5: Journaling My Emotions. March 30.

Just writing down what I feel, without judgment, is therapeutic. It's like unloading the mental baggage.

Journal Entry 6: Exercise Routine. April 7.

Today, I began a daily exercise routine. A 30-minute jog after work cleared my head and boosted my mood. I hadn't realized how much I missed physical activity. Here's to a healthier me!

Journal Entry 7: Connecting with Friends. April 15.

Met up with some old friends for a game night. It felt great to laugh and share stories. Reconnecting with my social support network is proving to be a crucial part of getting back on balance.

Journal Entry 8: Parenting Classes. April 25.

I signed up for a parenting class today. It's not about fixing what's wrong but learning new strategies. The first session was insightful, and it's reassuring to know I'm not alone in facing these challenges.

Journal Entry 9: Practicing Self-Compassion. May 2.

I've started being kinder to myself. Today, when I shouted at Tyler for smearing peanut butter on the sofa, I didn't beat myself up over it. Instead, I acknowledged it, learned from it, and moved on. Progress, not perfection, is the goal.

Journal Entry 10: Family Time. May 10.

Tonight, I decided to switch off all screens and spend quality time with the family. We played board games and told stories. It was a great reminder of why I'm on this healing journey—to be a better dad and make lasting memories with Jenny, Ashley, and Tyler (and who knows who else, lol).

KEY TAKEAWAYS

- Working too hard at parenting isn't good for you or your children.

- Your children's lives won't be ruined if you ignore them sometimes.
- Taking time for yourself keeps you around longer for your children.

As we conclude this journey, you should be well-equipped to handle all your toddler challenges and more. Remember, parenting is a marathon, not a sprint, and taking care of yourself is vital for your family.

Got a Minute?

No one denies that the toddler years are hard work, but they're also some of the most exciting and rewarding years of your parenting journey. Now that you're prepared for what lies ahead, why not take a moment to share that joy with other dads?

Simply by sharing your honest opinion of this book and a little about your own experience as a father, you'll help more men pass the toddler test with flying colors.

IN UNDER 1 MINUTE
YOU CAN HELP OTHERS JUST LIKE YOU BY LEAVING A REVIEW!

Thank you so much for your support. Enjoy this phase – let me tell you, it's a wild ride!

Scan the QR code here

CONCLUSION

I hope you now feel fully equipped to raise your toddler. Being a new dad means returning, through our children's eyes, to a world characterized by boundless energy, curious exploration, and constant wonder. We once lived in that world for all too short a time, but then we grew up. Our toddlers, who go through this rapid development, reawaken our own inner child.

I especially hope you now see parenting as the joyful journey it is and that any challenges are only part of what makes bringing up our children so meaningful. If I've left anything out, or if you have questions, write a review and post it on Amazon. I'll respond and address your concerns in the next edition of this book.

Toddlers, with their heightened mobility, growing self-awareness, and insatiable curiosity, are learning how to navigate the world around them. They are experiencing a profound and rapid phase of development and virtually drag us along for the ride. As parents, we want to guide them and protect them as best we can, which sometimes means—and this is the part that most parents fail to learn —not guiding them at all.

As a dad, your role is pivotal in nurturing your toddler's growth. In these pages, we've delved into the significance of Piaget's cognitive development stages, offering insights into why your toddler may sometimes seem far from angelic. These stages serve as a roadmap for comprehending the captivating yet occasionally bewildering twists and turns of your child's development.

Engaging in play and assisting your child in navigating their emotions are potent tools at your disposal. To beat this drum one last time, remember that making mistakes is an inevitable part of this journey, and your child won't be permanently scarred by your lapses in perfect *dadhood*. Showing you're a flawed human being better prepares them for life and an adult relationship with you in the future.

Perhaps the most important part of your father-child relationship is the conversations you will have. Your toddler is a linguistic sponge, absorbing words and concepts at a remarkable pace. Talking with them helps them develop empathy—a vital skill that will shape your child into a successful and compassionate adult.

When toddlers learn to talk, they also learn to argue. Tantrums, a natural component of a toddler's development, can be exasperating. Remember, you are not alone in confronting these challenges. Teach your toddler how to manage their emotions (ideally before they reach the age of four). With guidance and support, children can attain self-control, transforming these turbulent tantrums into valuable life lessons.

Part of teaching them such discipline involves having a structured daily routine that is adapted to both your family situation and your toddler's inherent temperament. It's crucial to understand that there is no one-size-fits-all approach. Choose the combination of techniques that best suits your toddler and aligns with your family's unique dynamics.

Also, even as you try to be the best possible parent, don't forget the importance of self-care. Adequate sleep is vital for maintaining your physical and mental well-being. A well-rested parent is better equipped to face the challenges of parenting a toddler with patience and resilience.

You will certainly need to be well-rested for potty training, which is often a parent's first encounter with their child's burgeoning independence. This is a step towards self-sufficiency, and remember, there's no need for strict timeframes. Patience is your ally here, and mastering your natural aversion to the messier aspects of this journey will make the task more manageable.

You should also encourage your toddler's newfound self-reliance by allowing them to take part in rule-setting. But when those boundaries are pushed, it's crucial to stand firm, imparting valuable lessons about responsibility and consequences.

Your relationship with your children is a source of profound meaning and purpose in your life and a treasure trove of memories in the making. Cherish every moment spent together, for these are the building blocks of their future. If you have more than one child, sibling rivalry, though not inevitable, may rear its head. Yet, with guidance and your calm intervention, it can be managed, ensuring a harmonious home.

Harmony, of course, requires a happy spouse. While the love for your children knows no bounds, it's essential not to lose sight of your relationship with your partner. Upholding the delicate balance between parental responsibilities and nurturing your connection is paramount. Relationships, like life itself, have their ups and downs, and it's vital to address challenges together.

Healthy relationships, as we've learned, thrive on more than just romance. Practical logistics play a significant role, requiring a well-thought-out plan and dedicated effort. Remember, working too hard at parenting can be detrimental to both you and your children. Occasional moments of "ignoring" them will not scar them for life but provide you with the necessary respite.

Taking time for yourself is not selfish but a way to ensure you're around longer for your children. Self-care is a crucial part of being a loving, present parent. As you navigate the intricate terrain of parenting toddlers, remember that it's not only about their growth but yours as well.

Being a dad is a thrilling, challenging, and profoundly rewarding journey. You've equipped yourself with the tools and insights in this book; now it's time to apply them. Embrace the joys, learn from the challenges, and grow with your child. Start today by selecting one strategy from each chapter and applying it this week. Your family's future awaits, and you're ready.

In closing, embrace the unique challenges and joys of parenting toddlers with an open heart and a willing spirit. Each day presents an opportunity to learn, grow, and bond with your child, creating memories that will accompany them into adulthood. Parenthood is a transformative journey, and you are equipped with the wisdom and resilience to navigate it with grace and love. May your days be filled with laughter, shared experiences, and the immeasurable joy that comes from being a dad.

NOTES

INTRODUCTION

1. PennState Extension. "Supporting Infant-Toddler Development." https://extension.psu.edu/programs/betterkidcare/news/supporting-infant-toddler-development.
2. Colorado Early Learning & Development Guidelines. "Infancy to Toddlerhood." https://earlylearningco.org/guidelines/transitions/typical-transitions/infancy-to-toddlerhood/.
3. "Infancy to Toddlerhood."

1. THE ADVENTURE OF RAISING A GROWING TODDLER

1. CDC. "Child Development: Toddlers (1-2 Years Old) | CDC." Centers for Disease Control and Prevention, November 7, 2019. https://www.cdc.gov/ncbddd/childdevelopment/positiveparenting/toddlers.html.
2. Philadelphia, The Children's Hospital of. "Developmental Milestones." Text, May 5, 2014. https://www.chop.edu/primary-care/developmental-milestones.
3. CDC, "Child Development."
4. Ph.D, Alicia Nortje. "Piaget's Stages: 4 Stages of Cognitive Development & Theory." PositivePsychology.com, May 3, 2021. https://positivepsychology.com/piaget-stages-theory/.
5. Dawes, Robyn. *House of Cards*. 1st edition. New York: Free Press, 1996.
6. Pinker, Steven. *The Blank Slate: The Modern Denial of Human Nature.* Reprint edition. London: Penguin Books, 2003.
7. Raising Children Network. "Emotions and Play: Toddlers," n.d. https://raisingchildren.net.au/toddlers/play-learning/play-toddler-development/emotions-play-toddlers.

8. "The Importance of Play: How Fathers Can Use Play to Promote Development | Fatherhood.Gov." Accessed November 11, 2023. http://www.fatherhood.gov/dadtalk-blog/importance-play-how-fathers-can-use-play-promote-development.

9. "The Benefits of Nurturing Care: How Early Interactions Influence Many Aspects of Our Development." First 1001 Day Movement, n.d.

10. "Epigenetics | Psychology Today." Accessed November 11, 2023. https://www.psychologytoday.com/us/basics/epigenetics.

11. Trzaskowski, Maciej, Philip S. Dale, and Robert Plomin. "No Genetic Influence for Childhood Behavior Problems from DNA Analysis." *Journal of the American Academy of Child and Adolescent Psychiatry* 52, no. 10 (October 2013): 1048-1056.e3. https://doi.org/10.1016/j.jaac.2013.07.016.

2. THE LANGUAGE OF LOVE

1. "Dick and Jane." In *Wikipedia*, October 11, 2023. https://en.wikipedia.org/w/index.php?title=Dick_and_Jane&oldid=1179603378.

2. Mental Floss. "15 Fun Facts About Dick and Jane</Em>," September 16, 2015. https://www.mentalfloss.com/article/68475/15-fun-facts-about-dick-and-jane.

3. "Key Words Reading Scheme." In *Wikipedia*, August 25, 2023. https://en.wikipedia.org/w/index.php?title=Key_Words_Reading_Scheme&oldid=1172182906.

4. Pinker, Steven. *The Language Instinct*. 1st ed. New York: W. Morrow and Co, 1994.

5. Toddler Talk. "2 Year Old Milestones - Speech & Language + Checklist," n.d. https://toddlertalk.com/blog/2-year-old-speech-checklist.

6. "2 Year Old Milestones - Speech & Language + Checklist."

7. Pinker, *The Language Instinct*, 278–79.

8. Goodstart Corporate. "Why Teaching Children Empathy Is More Important than Ever," February 22, 2018. https://www.goodstart.org.au/parenting/why-teaching-children-empathy-is-more-important-than-ever.

9. "Why Teaching Children Empathy Is More Important than Ever."

3. MELTDOWNS MADE MANAGEABLE

1. Watkins, Britney. *The Ultimate Guide To Parenting: How To Raise Children Without Screwing Them Up*. S.l.: CreateSpace Independent Publishing Platform, 2015.
2. Peterson, Jordan B. *12 Rules for Life: An Antidote to Chaos*. Later prt. edition. Toronto: Random House Canada, 2018.
3. Child Mind Institute. "Why Do Kids Have Tantrums and Meltdowns?" Accessed November 11, 2023. https://childmind.org/article/why-do-kids-have-tantrums-and-meltdowns/.
4. Kagan, Jerome. *The Human Spark: The Science of Human Development*. 1st edition. New York: Basic Books, 2013.
5. Peterson, *12 Rules for Life*, 134.
6. Mayo Clinic. "Tantrum Tips for Parents of Toddlers." Accessed November 12, 2023. https://www.mayoclinic.org/healthy-lifestyle/infant-and-toddler-health/in-depth/tantrum/art-20047845.
7. Peterson, *12 Rules for Life*.
8. Tufts Medical Center Community Care. "Temper Tantrums: Teaching Your Child Self-Calming Skills." Accessed November 12, 2023. https://hhma.org/healthadvisor/pa-temperta-pep/.
9. Liliana. "How To Create An Environment For Children To Thrive." Mighty Kids, September 28, 2021. https://mightykidsacademy.com/how-to-create-an-environment-for-children-to-thrive/.

4. SOLVING SLEEP WOES

1. Hopgood, Mei-Ling. *How Eskimos Keep Their Babies Warm: And Other Adventures in Parenting*. Algonquin Books, 2012.
2. Hopgood, *How Eskimos Keep Their Babies Warm*, 20.
3. Hopgood, *How Eskimos Keep Their Babies Warm*, 20.
4. "Childproofing and Preventing Household Accidents (for Parents) - Nemours KidsHealth," n.d. https://kidshealth.org/en/parents/childproof.html.

5. Mindell, Jodi A., and Ariel A. Williamson. "Benefits of a Bedtime Routine in Young Children: Sleep, Development, and Beyond." *Sleep Medicine Reviews* 40 (August 2018): 93–108. https://doi.org/10.1016/j.smrv.2017.10.007.

6. Verywell Family. "Review These Dos and Don'ts of a Good Bedtime Routine." Accessed November 12, 2023. https://www.verywellfamily.com/kids-and-bedtime-routines-2634260.

7. Happiest Baby. "Advice for Sleep Training Your Toddler." Accessed November 12, 2023. https://www.happiestbaby.com/blogs/toddler/toddler-sleep-training.

8. O'Shea, Elizabeth. "18 Tips for Parents to Get a Good Night's Sleep." *Parent 4 Success* (blog), March 8, 2012. https://www.parent4success.com/2012/03/08/18-tips-for-parents-to-get-a-good-nights-sleep/.

5. POTTY TRAINING LIKE A PRO

1. Hopgood, *How Eskimos Keep Their Babies Warm*, 83.

2. Hopgood, *How Eskimos Keep Their Babies Warm*, 96.

3. "Tips for Toilet Training a Baby - SuperBottoms," n.d. https://superbottoms.com/blogs/baby-care/importance-of-toilet-training.

4. "Toilet Training (for Parents) - Nemours KidsHealth," n.d. https://kidshealth.org/en/parents/toilet-teaching.html.

5. "Ways To Make Potty Training Fun | Pull-Ups® US," n.d. https://www.pull-ups.com/en-us/resources/tips-advice/how-to-potty-train/how-to-make-potty-training-fun.

6. Hopgood, *How Eskimos Keep Their Babies Warm*, 89.

7. DiaperFreeBaby. "Making EC as Easy as 1,2, Pee!," n.d. http://diaperfreebaby.org/practicing-ec/ec-basics/making-ec-as-easy-as-12-pee/.

8. Healthline. "Elimination Communication: Definition, Benefits, and Drawbacks," September 20, 2019. https://www.healthline.com/health/parenting/elimination-communication.

6. RAISING A FREE SPIRIT WITHIN SAFE BOUNDARIES

1. ESMS. "The Importance of Boundaries," December 1, 2021. https://www.esms.org.uk/news/importance-boundaries.
2. Peterson, *12 Rules for Life*.
3. Hill, Chase. *Healthy Boundaries: How to Set Strong Boundaries, Say No Without Guilt, and Maintain Good Relationships With Your Parents, Family, and Friends.* June 21, 2021), 2021.
4. Hill, *Healthy Boundaries*.
5. Growing Early Minds. "How to Set Healthy Boundaries with Your Kids," November 5, 2019. https://growingearlyminds.org.au/tips/how-to-set-healthy-boundaries-with-your-kids/.
6. "How to Discipline Your Child the Smart and Healthy Way | UNICEF Parenting," n.d. https://www.unicef.org/parenting/child-care/how-discipline-your-child-smart-and-healthy-way.
7. "How to Discipline Your Child the Smart and Healthy Way | UNICEF Parenting."
8. "Why It's Important to Give Your Toddler Choices," n.d. https://babysparks.com/2021/01/27/why-its-important-to-give-your-toddler-choices/.

7. A DAD'S GUIDE TO A CLOSE-KNIT FAMILY

1. Peoplemag. "Michael J. Fox's 4 Kids: Everything to Know," n.d. https://people.com/parents/all-about-michael-j-fox-kids/.
2. Scarlet. "10 Benefits of Spending Time With Family." Family Focus Blog, February 24, 2021. https://familyfocusblog.com/6-benefits-of-spending-time-together-as-a-family/.
3. Raeburn, Paul. *[Do Fathers Matter?: What Science Is Telling Us About the Parent We've Overlooked]*, n.d.
4. Raising Children Network. "Relationships and Child Development," n.d. https://raisingchildren.net.au/newborns/development/understanding-development/relationships-development.

5. "Relationships and Child Development."
6. MedicineNet. "What Are the Main Causes of Sibling Rivalry?," n.d. https://www.medicinenet.com/what_are_the_main_causes_of_sibling_rivalry/article.htm.

8. PARENTING WITHOUT LOSING EACH OTHER

1. Services, Department of Health & Human. "Relationships and Communication," n.d. http://www.betterhealth.vic.gov.au/health/healthyliving/relationships-and-communication.
2. Benson, Kyle. "The Magic Relationship Ratio, According to Science." The Gottman Institute, October 4, 2017. https://www.gottman.com/blog/the-magic-relationship-ratio-according-science/.
3. Greater Good. "Getting the Ratios Right," n.d. https://greatergood.berkeley.edu/article/item/getting_the_ratios_right.
4. Benson, "The Magic Relationship Ratio, According to Science."
5. BabyCenter. "Dividing Childcare and Housework Duties with Your Partner," n.d. https://www.babycenter.com/family/house-and-home/dividing-childcare-and-housework-duties-with-your-partner_446.
6. Oxford Reference. "John Churton Collins," n.d. https://doi.org/10.1093/oi/authority.20110803095624566.
7. Dadula, Airyl Marie. "12 Ways to Support Each Other in a Relationship," March 13, 2018. https://inspiringtips.com/ways-to-support-each-other-in-a-relationship/.

9. RECHARGING THE DAD BATTERY

1. Staff, Newport Academy. "Identifying Signs and Symptoms of Parental Burnout." Newport Academy (blog), August 19, 2022. https://www.newportacademy.com/resources/restoring-families/parental-burnout/.

2. Roskam, Isabelle, Joyce Aguiar, Ege Akgun, Gizem Arikan, Mariana Artavia, Hervé Avalosse, Kaisa Aunola, et al. "Parental Burnout Around the Globe: A 42-Country Study." *Affective Science* 2, no. 1 (2021): 58–79. https://doi.org/10.1007/s42761-020-00028-4.

3. Roskam et al., "Parental Burnout Around the Globe."

4. Roskam et al., "Parental Burnout Around the Globe."

5. "The Impact of Parental Burnout," n.d. https://www.apa.org/monitor/2021/10/cover-parental-burnout.

6. Contributor, Mommy. "11 Self Care Tips for New Dads to Conquer the Daddy Blues," September 9, 2022. https://tajthings.com/self-care-tips-for-new-dads/.

7. Dad On The Move Family Travel Blog. "8 Reasons Why Having Me-Time Should Be Part of Every Dad's Healthy Habits," n.d. https://www.ivankhristravels.com/2020/09/me-time.html.

REFERENCES

Abuse, National Institute on Drug. "New NIH Study Reveals Shared Genetic Markers Underlying Substance Use Disorders | National Institute on Drug Abuse (NIDA)," March 22, 2023. https://nida.nih. gov/news-events/news-releases/2023/03/new-nih-study-reveals-shared-genetic-markers-underlying-substance-use-disorders.

Azeredo, Andreia, Diana Moreira, Patrícia Figueiredo, and Fernando Barbosa. "Delinquent Behavior: Systematic Review of Genetic and Environmental Risk Factors." *Clinical Child and Family Psychology Review* 22, no. 4 (December 2019): 502–26. https://doi.org/10. 1007/s10567-019-00298-w.

BabyCenter. "Dividing Childcare and Housework Duties with Your Partner," n.d. https://www.babycenter.com/family/house-and-home/dividing-childcare-and-housework-duties-with-your-part ner_446.

Benson, Kyle. "The Magic Relationship Ratio, According to Science." The Gottman Institute, October 4, 2017. https://www.gottman. com/blog/the-magic-relationship-ratio-according-science/.

———. "The Magic Relationship Ratio, According to Science." The Gottman Institute, October 4, 2017. https://www.gottman.com/ blog/the-magic-relationship-ratio-according-science/.

CDC. "Child Development: Toddlers (1-2 Years Old) | CDC." Centers for Disease Control and Prevention, November 7, 2019. https:// www.cdc.gov/ncbddd/childdevelopment/positiveparenting/ toddlers.html.

Child Mind Institute. "Why Do Kids Have Tantrums and Meltdowns?" Accessed November 11, 2023. https://childmind.org/article/why-do-kids-have-tantrums-and-meltdowns/.

"Childproofing and Preventing Household Accidents (for Parents) - Nemours KidsHealth," n.d. https://kidshealth.org/en/parents/child proof.html.

Colorado Early Learning & Development Guidelines. "Infancy to

Toddlerhood." Accessed November 10, 2023. https://earlylearn
ingco.org/guidelines/transitions/typical-transitions/infancy-to-
toddlerhood/.

Contributor, Mommy. "11 Self Care Tips for New Dads to Conquer
the Daddy Blues," September 9, 2022. https://tajthings.com/self-
care-tips-for-new-dads/.

Dad On The Move Family Travel Blog. "8 Reasons Why Having Me-
Time Should Be Part of Every Dad's Healthy Habits," n.d. https://
www.ivankhristravels.com/2020/09/me-time.html.

Dadula, Airyl Marie. "12 Ways to Support Each Other in a Relationship," March 13, 2018. https://inspiringtips.com/ways-to-support-
each-other-in-a-relationship/.

Dawes, Robyn. *House of Cards*. 1st edition. New York: Free Press, 1996.

DiaperFreeBaby. "Making EC as Easy as 1,2, Pee!," n.d. http://diaper
freebaby.org/practicing-ec/ec-basics/making-ec-as-easy-as-12-
pee/.

"Dick and Jane." In *Wikipedia*, October 11, 2023. https://en.wikipedia.
org/w/index.php?title=Dick_and_Jane&oldid=1179603378.

Elizabeth. "45+ Insightful & Funny Quotes About Toddlers." Shoestring
Baby. Last modified September 14, 2023. https://shoestringbaby.
com/quotes-about-toddlers/ .

"Epigenetics | Psychology Today." Accessed November 11, 2023.
https://www.psychologytoday.com/us/basics/epigenetics.

ESMS. "The Importance of Boundaries," December 1, 2021. https://
www.esms.org.uk/news/importance-boundaries.

Goodstart Corporate. "Why Teaching Children Empathy Is More
Important than Ever," February 22, 2018. https://www.goodstart.
org.au/parenting/why-teaching-children-empathy-is-more-impor
tant-than-ever.

Greater Good. "Getting the Ratios Right," n.d. https://greatergood.
berkeley.edu/article/item/getting_the_ratios_right.

Growing Early Minds. "How to Set Healthy Boundaries with Your
Kids," November 5, 2019. https://growingearlyminds.org.au/tips/
how-to-set-healthy-boundaries-with-your-kids/.

Happiest Baby. "Advice for Sleep Training Your Toddler." Accessed
November 12, 2023. https://www.happiestbaby.com/blogs/

toddler/toddler-sleep-training.

Healthline. "Elimination Communication: Definition, Benefits, and Drawbacks," September 20, 2019. https://www.healthline.com/health/parenting/elimination-communication.

Hill, Chase. *Healthy Boundaries: How to Set Strong Boundaries, Say No Without Guilt, and Maintain Good Relationships With Your Parents, Family, and Friends.* June 21, 2021), 2021.

Hopgood, Mei-Ling. *How Eskimos Keep Their Babies Warm: And Other Adventures in Parenting.* Algonquin Books, 2012.

"How to Discipline Your Child the Smart and Healthy Way | UNICEF Parenting," n.d. https://www.unicef.org/parenting/child-care/how-discipline-your-child-smart-and-healthy-way.

https://www.apa.org. "The Impact of Parental Burnout," n.d. https://www.apa.org/monitor/2021/10/cover-parental-burnout.

Kagan, Jerome. *The Human Spark: The Science of Human Development.* 1st edition. New York: Basic Books, 2013.

"Key Words Reading Scheme." In *Wikipedia*, August 25, 2023. https://en.wikipedia.org/w/index.php?title=Key_Words_Reading_Scheme&oldid=1172182906.

Liliana. "How To Create An Environment For Children To Thrive." Mighty Kids, September 28, 2021. https://mightykidsacademy.com/how-to-create-an-environment-for-children-to-thrive/.

London, University College. "A Parent's Genes Can Influence a Child's Educational Success, Inherited or Not," n.d. https://medicalxpress.com/news/2021-08-parent-genes-child-success-inherited.html.

Mayo Clinic. "Tantrum Tips for Parents of Toddlers." Accessed November 12, 2023. https://www.mayoclinic.org/healthy-lifestyle/infant-and-toddler-health/in-depth/tantrum/art-20047845.

MedicineNet. "What Are the Main Causes of Sibling Rivalry?," n.d. https://www.medicinenet.com/what_are_the_main_causes_of_sibling_rivalry/article.htm.

Mental Floss. "15 Fun Facts About Dick and Jane</Em>," September 16, 2015. https://www.mentalfloss.com/article/68475/15-fun-facts-about-dick-and-jane.

Mindell, Jodi A., and Ariel A. Williamson. "Benefits of a Bedtime Routine in Young Children: Sleep, Development, and Beyond." *Sleep*

Medicine Reviews 40 (August 2018): 93–108. https://doi.org/10. 1016/j.smrv.2017.10.007.

O'Shea, Elizabeth. "18 Tips for Parents to Get a Good Night's Sleep." *Parent 4 Success* (blog), March 8, 2012. https://www.parent4success. com/2012/03/08/18-tips-for-parents-to-get-a-good-nights-sleep/.

Oxford Reference. "John Churton Collins," n.d. https://doi.org/10. 1093/oi/authority.20110803095624566.

PennState Extension. "Supporting Infant-Toddler Development," n.d. https://extension.psu.edu/programs/betterkidcare/news/support ing-infant-toddler-development.

Peoplemag. "Michael J. Fox's 4 Kids: Everything to Know," n.d. https:// people.com/parents/all-about-michael-j-fox-kids/.

Peterson, Jordan B. *12 Rules for Life: An Antidote to Chaos.* Later prt. edition. Toronto: Random House Canada, 2018.

Ph.D, Alicia Nortje. "Piaget's Stages: 4 Stages of Cognitive Development & Theory." PositivePsychology.com, May 3, 2021. https://posi tivepsychology.com/piaget-stages-theory/.

Philadelphia, The Children's Hospital of. "Developmental Milestones." Text, May 5, 2014. https://www.chop.edu/primary-care/develop mental-milestones.

Pinker, Steven. *The Blank Slate: The Modern Denial of Human Nature.* Reprint edition. London: Penguin Books, 2003.

———. *The Language Instinct.* 1st ed. New York: W. Morrow and Co, 1994.

Raeburn, Paul. *[Do Fathers Matter?: What Science Is Telling Us About the Parent We've Overlooked]*, n.d.

Raising Children Network. "Emotions and Play: Toddlers," n.d. https:// raisingchildren.net.au/toddlers/play-learning/play-toddler-develop ment/emotions-play-toddlers.

Raising Children Network. "Relationships and Child Development," n.d. https://raisingchildren.net.au/newborns/development/under standing-development/relationships-development.

Roskam, Isabelle, Joyce Aguiar, Ege Akgun, Gizem Arikan, Mariana Artavia, Hervé Avalosse, Kaisa Aunola, et al. "Parental Burnout Around the Globe: A 42-Country Study." *Affective Science* 2, no. 1 (2021): 58–79. https://doi.org/10.1007/s42761-020-00028-4.

Scarlet. "10 Benefits of Spending Time With Family." Family Focus Blog, February 24, 2021. https://familyfocusblog.com/6-benefits-of-spending-time-together-as-a-family/.

Services, Department of Health & Human. "Relationships and Communication," n.d. http://www.betterhealth.vic.gov.au/health/healthyliving/relationships-and-communication.

———. "Relationships and Communication." Accessed November 13, 2023. http://www.betterhealth.vic.gov.au/health/healthyliving/relationships-and-communication.

Staff, Newport Academy. "Identifying Signs and Symptoms of Parental Burnout." *Newport Academy* (blog), August 19, 2022. https://www.newportacademy.com/resources/restoring-families/parental-burnout/.

"The Benefits of Nurturing Care: How Early Interactions Influence Many Aspects of Our Development." First 1001 Day Movement, n.d.

"The Importance of Play: How Fathers Can Use Play to Promote Development | Fatherhood.Gov." Accessed November 11, 2023. http://www.fatherhood.gov/dadtalk-blog/importance-play-how-fathers-can-use-play-promote-development.

"Tips for Toilet Training a Baby - SuperBottoms," n.d. https://superbottoms.com/blogs/baby-care/importance-of-toilet-training.

Toddler Talk. "2 Year Old Milestones - Speech & Language + Checklist," n.d. https://toddlertalk.com/blog/2-year-old-speech-checklist.

"Toilet Training (for Parents) - Nemours KidsHealth," n.d. https://kidshealth.org/en/parents/toilet-teaching.html.

Trzaskowski, Maciej, Philip S. Dale, and Robert Plomin. "No Genetic Influence for Childhood Behavior Problems from DNA Analysis." *Journal of the American Academy of Child and Adolescent Psychiatry* 52, no. 10 (October 2013): 1048-1056.e3. https://doi.org/10.1016/j.jaac.2013.07.016.

Tufts Medical Center Community Care. "Temper Tantrums: Teaching Your Child Self-Calming Skills." Accessed November 12, 2023. https://hhma.org/healthadvisor/pa-temperta-pep/.

Verywell Family. "Review These Dos and Don'ts of a Good Bedtime

Routine." Accessed November 12, 2023. https://www.verywellfam ily.com/kids-and-bedtime-routines-2634260.

Watkins, Britney. *The Ultimate Guide To Parenting: How To Raise Children Without Screwing Them Up.* S.l.: CreateSpace Independent Publishing Platform, 2015.

"Ways To Make Potty Training Fun | Pull-Ups® US," n.d. https://www. pull-ups.com/en-us/resources/tips-advice/how-to-potty-train/ how-to-make-potty-training-fun.

"Why It's Important to Give Your Toddler Choices," n.d. https:// babysparks.com/2021/01/27/why-its-important-to-give-your-toddler-choices/.